ORGAN GRINDER

ORGAN GRINDER

A CLASSICAL EDUCATION
GONE ASTRAY

ALAN FISHBONE

FARRAR, STRAUS AND GIROUX   NEW YORK

Farrar, Straus and Giroux
18 West 18th Street, New York 10011

Printed in the United States of America
First edition, 2017

Library of Congress Cataloging-in-Publication Data
Names: Fishbone, Alan, author.
Title: Organ grinder : a classical education gone astray / Alan
    Fishbone.
Description: New York : FSG Originals, 2017.
Identifiers: LCCN 2016027559 | ISBN 9780865478343 (paperback) |
    ISBN 9780374713683 (ebook)
Subjects: LCSH: Mortality. | Freedom. | Motorcycling. | BISAC:
    PHILOSOPHY / History & Surveys / Ancient & Classical. |
    TRANSPORTATION / Motorcycles / General.
Classification: LCC PS3606.I76848 O74 2017 | DDC 814/.6—dc23
LC record available at https://lccn.loc.gov/2016027559

Designed by Jonathan D. Lippincott

Our books may be purchased in bulk for promotional, educational,
or business use. Please contact your local bookseller or the
Macmillan Corporate and Premium Sales Department
at 1-800-221-7945, extension 5442, or by e-mail at
MacmillanSpecialMarkets@macmillan.com.

www.fsgbooks.com • www.fsgoriginals.com
www.twitter.com/fsgbooks • www.facebook.com/fsgbooks

1 3 5 7 9 10 8 6 4 2

γνῶθι σεαυτόν

παραχαράσσειν τό νόμισμα

Know yourself and deface the currency: two Pythian proverbs. And the latter means, scorn common opinion and value truth over the moral coin of the masses.

—Suda

PART I

It was customary in an ancient work of poetry for the writer to announce his purpose at the beginning, to tell you what the book's about, so you, the reader, or listener most likely, could decide whether to stick around and see if it turns out to be interesting, or decide no, this looks like a waste of time, I guess I'll be out of here. Depending on the genre, there might be an invocation to the Muses or a brownnosing dedication to a rich patron, maybe a complaint about a woman or the decadence of the times, but both reader and writer would know what to expect: action, comedy, romance, maybe even some philosophy; how much violence, adult language, or nudity it might contain; whether just a few tits and asses here and there, or some hard-core pornography, gay or straight, high or low, tragic, comic, etc. . . . The tone would be a signal as well: salty or pretentious, arrogant or hesitant, light, graphic, and so on. The prologue was like a movie preview, you could tell right away what you were getting. Here you're going to get a bit of everything, some motorcycles, some freedom, some mortality, and some ancient Greek philosophy. One of my favorite ancient writers is the satirist Horace, who wrote about anything, meandering from high to low, changing the tone whenever the material required. He has a sincere irony that makes it hard to tell sometimes if he's joking or serious, but it doesn't matter. He always tries to be graceful and entertaining. I'm going to copy him a little, or at least try to follow his lead, so think of this book as a ride if you can, free to go where it pleases.

Think *Easy Rider*, rolling along in the West. It's 1969 and two hippie bikers, Wyatt Earp and Billy the Kid, are flush with cash from a cocaine deal. They ride around on a couple of beautiful Panheads, loosely bound for New Orleans, with the coke money stashed in a plastic tube in Wyatt's gas tank. The gas tank is painted the stars and stripes of the American flag. "Born to Be Wild" plays over spectacular vistas of red desert sandstone, flaming sunsets, dappled, soft-focus, forest-filtered sunbeams, their long hair blowing in the wind. Wyatt and Billy are perfect Platonic icons of biker freedom. They ride around, meet different people, take different drugs, visit a commune, a brothel, a diner, a ranch, an acid trip blur in a New Orleans graveyard. They just want to be free to ride their bikes "without getting hassled by the Man." And that's it: the idea and emblem, a platinum-plated American cliché.

They get arrested and pick up an alcoholic lawyer played by Jack Nicholson, who decides to ride along for a while in a rumpled suit and his old high school football helmet. One night by a campfire, he and a jittery, bug-eyed Dennis Hopper have the following conversation:

"You know this used to be a hell of a good country. I can't understand what's gone wrong with it."

"Man, everybody got chicken, that's what happened. Hey, we can't even get into like a second-rate hotel—I mean a second-rate motel, you dig? People think we're gonna cut their throat or something, man. They're scared, man."

"Oh, they're not scared of you. They're scared of what you represent to 'em."

"Hey, man, all we represent to them, man, is somebody who needs a haircut."

"Oh, no. What you represent to them is freedom."

"What the hell's wrong with freedom, man? That's what it's all about!"

"Oh yeah, that's right, that's what it's all about, all right. But talking about it and being it, that's two different things. I mean, it's real hard to be free when you are bought and sold in the marketplace. 'Course, don't ever tell any-body that they're not free 'cause then they're gonna get real busy killing and maiming to prove to you that they are. Oh yeah. They're gonna talk to you and talk to you and talk to you about individual freedom, but they see a free individual, it's gonna scare 'em."

And this turns out to be prophetic, because in the end all three of them are murdered: the lawyer beaten to death in his sleep; Billy and Wyatt killed over nothing, by a pair of stereotyped rednecks, with stupid, ignorant grins, cruising around in a rickety old pickup. They're shot and left bleeding in the road. The star-spangled gas tank full of coke money explodes in flames, unfurling like fingers of napalm. No more freedom, man—the sixties are over, like the blown-out skull of John F. Kennedy. Malcolm X, Che Guevara, Fred Hampton, Martin Luther King Jr. The Man has won.

But at least there's still the icon of the biker in glorious flight, free, "freedom," people always use that word, about America, about motorcycles, especially people who don't ride them. They say, "It must be great to have a bike, man, the freedom"—things like that. I've heard it a million times. And riding through a piece of arid Wyoming moon, for example, or even just to the beach, out of the city, on a scorched blur of road that stretches into the horizon and disappears—you do feel free. The hot wind blows through your face and hair, and you're an angel in flight, with no mission other than to fly. The past, the future, yourself—it all falls away, like you're even free from time. It's a complete feeling. I know that might sound a little silly, or grandiose even, and it is, but people who ride motorcycles are willing to risk their lives for that feeling. It's like a sacrament, and once you have it, it's hard to live without. And like a sacrament, it can be true or false—a pleasure that takes you out of the world for a while, a transubstantiation, or the ultimate cliché of testosterone and posturing, pure male vanity. It's bullshit and a miracle at the same time. I've lost a couple of friends from bike accidents, and I walked away from one of my own that should have killed me, caused mostly by my own arrogance and stupidity. It's nothing but luck that I'm still here. I've known others who were better riders and less stupid than I am who are gone.

Maybe that's part of the reason for all the skulls and skeletons in the tattoos and imagery around bikes, that death is always there, all around us, for everyone—just with bikes it's a little more obvious, but we're all the same, dry skeletons under wet flesh for a limited amount of time. Horace says "the years slip by," carpe diem, memento mori: What do you want here before you go down below? Not to heaven or hell: for him there are no such fantasies—just here and now. He says let's drink and savor the time. I don't know if riding a motorcycle is freedom or pleasure, or how to tell the difference between those two half the time. Maybe that's all freedom means—not having to do what you don't want to do, and being able to do what you do, freedom from and freedom to, whether to pray or fuck or sit around in the sun, freedom for yourself or even from yourself, not to be bothered, harassed, or killed, just to be left alone. It's not much of an idea, really, a kind of hedonistic tautology, but even so, it seems so difficult to find. In a lost work titled *On Pleasure*, the ancient philosopher Heracleides of Pontus wrote that pleasure is the proper pursuit of free men because it relaxes and increases the soul. But by free men, he didn't mean people who had to work for a living, or women, or slaves—by far the majority—so how much of what he says is relevant? Or likewise what any of the ancients say? Aren't such maxims just the fossils of an extinct imperialist, pagan slave society?

A COUPLE OF QUESTIONS

I'll get on with it, but first I have a couple of questions that bother me, that are always lurking around in the background. Like, what about all this NSA and Homeland Security surveillance? Does it make you feel safe? Or is it true what Billy said in the movie: Did we all get chicken? For me the answers are yes, maybe we did get chicken, and no, it doesn't make me feel safe. I feel like my freedom is being taken away while I'm not paying attention, one little thing at a time. The Fourth Amendment, habeas corpus, voter fraud, stellar wind. That I'm being lied to and spied on and know it, but am mysteriously numb and paralyzed, as if I've been poisoned. The thought that those anonymous gray men in cheap black suits and crew cuts can monitor people's phones and computers, and frame anyone they want to as a terrorist, makes me fear the government more than any shadowy terrorist boogeyman. I want gas for my bike, but I don't want to get spied on: Are those things really incompatible? Do people need to be kept in slavery or bombed into dust so I can enjoy my gas and ride? Sometimes I wonder if my bike is my price; as long as I have one and access to that pleasure, I'm acquiescent to the bigger picture; the surveillance, the killing. What does it have to do with me? I might not want to admit it, but my behavior seems to say, fuck the world, fuck global warming, fuck everybody. It's all too late. It'll all be over soon. Grab what you can. This is where karma put me, on the luckier side of things. Should I feel guilty that I'm not some kid in Iraq with his arms and legs blown off? Can't I just live my own life and try to be free? But it nags me when I pay my taxes—that I'm complicit in the murder of children, that I'm feeding those monstrous corporations, that I am docile and submissive. Am I an accomplice or just another phony? What are you supposed to do?

To protest his own government's encroachments, in 2013 a Russian artist named Pyotr Pavlensky stripped himself naked and nailed his scrotum to the pavement of Red Square in Moscow, right in front of Lenin's tomb. You can see pictures and video of him on the Internet. He's thin and wiry, with a bony, ascetic face, mournful sunken eyes, and a shaved head, sitting on the ground with a gleaming silver nail driven through his pink scrotum into the dark gray stone. He performed this action on a holiday known as Police Day, though the police didn't seem to understand what he was doing or even know whether it was illegal. They covered him with a blanket to protect the public from the sight of his genitals, and called an ambulance. Then they pried the nail out, hauled him off to the station, and later released him. Pavlensky called this act "Fixation" and said of it, "a naked artist, looking at his testicles nailed to the cobblestone is a metaphor of the apathy, political indifference, and fatalism of modern Russian society. The government wants to turn people into safe and secure, gutless cattle, which are allowed only to work, consume and multiply. We're heading towards a police state . . . and ordinary people are allowing this to happen." There were different reviews in the media, some critics and journalists placing him in traditions of Actionism or self-immolation, likening him to the Desert Fathers or medieval flagellants. They mentioned people like Günter Brus, for example, who in 1968 at the University of Vienna stripped himself naked, cut himself with a razor, then pissed in a glass and drank it, smeared his body with shit, and sang the Austrian national anthem while masturbating. He was arrested and did six months in jail for "degrading state symbols." They compared Pavlensky to Joseph Beuys, who made furniture from the excess human fat of the imperial world and wrote, "he who can live care-free and sleep peacefully knowing that two thirds of humanity are hungry or dying of starvation while a large portion of the well-fed third must take slimming . . . to stay alive . . . ld* ask himself what kind of man he is and whether, moreover, he is a man at all."

I loved Pavlensky's gesture for its deliberate futility—how it seemed both selfless and narcissistic at the same time, and like a parody of crucifixion, as if he were saying you can't do anything, but you have to do something; either way they've got you by the balls. But what would it accomplish, really, to nail your balls into Ground Zero to protest the Patriot Act, or to the Western Wall in Jerusalem for the depredation of Palestine? It might make a nice selfie or brief meme before merging into the sludge of used information, but then what? Is it worth getting arrested for?

---

*These words were written in chalk on a blackboard and smudged away in a few places. It's a historical peculiarity that Beuys at the age of twelve was present at a Nazi book burning and rescued a copy of Linnaeus's zoological tract *Systema Naturae* from the flames.

TRUE SKETCH OF A MALE FANTASY

Summer afternoon. I rode past my friend Gigi's place of work. Gigi is a beautiful blond woman, forty-five, an actress, a yoga instructor, a spiritual therapist with a deep and zany sense of humor. She has a wide face, with big blue eyes, a gap-toothed smile, and an easy, old-fashioned glamour that gives her the look of a forties starlet. Somehow she manages to be both sultry and childlike at the same time. But she's a little bored, like she doesn't really know what she wants in this world, whether nothing or everything. She doesn't want a husband or even a boyfriend, but she likes sex a lot, and she's picky. "Most men bore me," she'll say, "they're so needy and insecure. Right away they're all over me, like a cheap suit, you know? Clingy, trying to control things. Or they're selfish and vain, like you are, just looking for a little wham, bam, thank you, ma'am, and then gone till the next time they feel like calling you.

It's amazing. It's like nobody has any manners anymore? I don't know why I like you, but I do. At least you're funny. And I do like riding around on that bike of yours. I just want you for sex too anyway, so there's a little taste of your own medicine for you. Some companionship is nice, maybe for a night or so, but that's it. Once a week would be perfect. I don't have time for anything more, at least not until my daughter's out of the house. Seems like a perfect arrangement to me."

We've known each other on and off for years but it had been a while since we'd seen each other.

She must have heard my bike go by or seen me out the window, because about twenty minutes later, she sent me a text that read:

Someone ought to do a study on the female response to the sound of a harley

I typed back:

Why? What's yours?

Pelvic floor awareness, release of oxytocin,*
slight wetness, possible increase in heart
rate . . . irritability.

---

*Oxford English Dictionary:

oxytocin: A mammalian pituitary hormone that stimulates contraction of the smooth muscle of the uterus and the milk ducts.

That would be a good study. I'd participate.
I bet harley might even sponsor it. Imagine the
advertising potential. Nothing wets a woman
like a hog . . . but why irritability?

Oh, hot and bothered like. Just fuckin pavlov's
dog really, nothing special. How about
you, dog, getting scratched behind your ears?

No, not really. Been a little slow lately.
Would you like to go for a ride, gg?

You know I would.

I picked her up a couple of hours later, after work, just
before twilight. I love that moment, in the long days of
summer, when the sky goes purple-blue and the heat
and traffic slowly relax into evening. It's almost like the
city is sighing.

Gigi was dressed in skintight light denim jeans that
grasped her curves like a glove and a skimpy tank top
tracing the silhouettes of her nipples and ribs in its light,
snug fabric. Her hair was braided into girlish pigtails.
She looked like a textbook sexual cliché, the "hot little
blonde," and she knew it. We both did. I just wanted to
rip her clothes off, lick her up and down, and screw
her. And she wanted that too. We were both stereo-
types: horny biker and saucy blonde, like characters out
of a tattoo. Live to ride, ride to live. A pair of skeletons,
dancing bones akimbo, drinking martinis.

We went for a drive out of Manhattan, through the Battery Tunnel, to the BQE, over the Gowanus and the long straightaway through Industry City and Sunset Park, then out along the bay and under the Verrazano Bridge, which glimmered in the twilight air like an ancient wonder. The bay was a heavy, luminous silver. It was so beautiful, and I was so happy to be moving like that through the warm air, with Gigi wedged up against me, the V of her crotch and her breasts grazing my back, a simple, material, worldly physical pleasure. The vibration of the engine was turning her on and before long Gigi was squirming forward on the seat and rubbing herself into me, reaching around my waist and squeezing, clicking her helmet into mine like a flirtatious bird. A warm throb began to push against the front of my jeans.

After a while, we couldn't take it anymore. I took her to a discreet little motel where you can rent a room for a few hours of anonymous seclusion. Sign your name as Jesse James and get a three-pack of condoms from the candy machine in the lobby. We got a tiny cubicle with mirrors everywhere and an enormous bed that took up almost the whole room. A clumsy fresco of clouds and blue sky on the ceiling, plexiglass panels around the bed, and closed-circuit porn on TV. We jumped on the bed and stripped each other's clothes off.

At some point I happened to catch sight of us in a long mirror on the back of the bathroom door. Gigi was standing and leaning forward on her arms, her back arched and her head tilted backward, her face a squinting mask of ecstasy. I was behind her with my arms clasped around her sides and my hands cupping her breasts from below, my face in her hair, humping her doggy style. When I saw that, it hit me how funny that word is—"hump"—its comical accuracy. My lower back was curled around her as I thrust my hips up and forward in that same exaggerated curl of a dog hunched in the street around a slowly emerging turd, and looking off in the distance, slightly ashamed. There I was, fixed in the mirror: a humpbacked satyr, pumping away with his flagrant lipstick wiener. Satyr and nymph in the grove of a cheap motel.

We changed positions and moved around to different corners of the bed, probing and enjoying, licking and moaning. I sucked her vagina for a while, snuffling in its musky tang, massaged her, pressing my thumbs into the flexed muscles of her shoulders as I slid in and out from behind. Her anus looked like a large pink raisin. My penis seemed like a hand, or a blind neuron, reaching into her and grasping at something unknown, transmitting it back to the brain in waves of dopamine. I found myself looking into the same mirror again. This time Gigi was on her hands and knees stretched forward before me in a blowjob. I watched her from behind, the edges of her blond hair fluttering like a halo* as her head bobbed up and down in slow rhythms.

---

*"Halo," another beautiful word. The *OED* says,

> Greek ἅλως threshing-floor, disk of the sun, moon, or a shield.
>   1. a. A circle of light, either white or prismatically coloured, seen round a luminous body and caused by the refraction of light

17

Her shoulders and sinuous sides tapering down to slender hips and the rise of her luminous ass, the mesmerizing dark where it spread downward and split into a mossy mound of vulva. Such a beautiful body, the eternal, beautiful, naked female body. Her mouth's warm suction and her moving tongue made me close my eyes, and I could feel them rubbing against their eyelids as my head swayed backward and forward like a palm. I was gone. I didn't know who I was anymore, just gusts and gasps of pleasure blown across a shore.

---

through vapour; *spec.* that seen round the sun or moon, commonly of 22 or 46 degrees radius, with the red extremity of the spectrum inside the circle.

c. A coloured circle, such as those around the nipples, and those which surround vesicles or pustules; 1706 *Phillips's New World of Words* (ed. 6) Halo, or Halos . . . also a reddish Spot or Circle of Flesh which encompasses each Nipple in the Breasts of Women.

2. The circle or disk of light with which the head is surrounded in representations of Christ and the Saints; a nimbus.

3. *fig.* The ideal glory with which a person or thing is invested when viewed under the influence of feeling or sentiment.

CHARACTER, A SUTURE SUTRA

In its present incarnation, my nose looks something like a potato, a scarred brown lump that sits crooked between my cheekbones. It wasn't always like that, but about ten years ago, I smashed it in a motorcycle accident while wearing one of those flimsy plastic skullcaps they call a brain bucket, so my face was exposed when I hit. I was drunk and crashed into the back of a construction compressor that somehow had been left in the road on a spiraling exit ramp at three in the morning in Queens. The impact hurled me several feet into the air, projecting me miraculously over the compressor and onto my face on a grassy patch of roadside scrub. If I'd hit the compressor directly, my thorax would have been crushed and I would have died from internal injuries. And if I'd landed on asphalt, my face would have been torn off my skull like cheese from a pizza. I don't like to think about it. Well, they say that

God protects fools and drunkards. As it is, I broke my nose, tore my left biceps, and herniated a cervical disc. The bike, a '97 Ducati Monster 750, was totaled.

I lost consciousness. When I came to, I was strapped to a gurney in an ambulance on the way to Jamaica Hospital. My neck was in a brace and I was covered in blood. An EMT was peering into my dazed head with a pinpoint flashlight beam and trying to gauge the damage. Was I there? Could I tell him what day of the week it was? My name? When we got to the emergency room, they cut me out of my blood-drenched jacket, injected my face with anesthesia, began cleaning and stitching up my nose and forehead. I could feel the friction of the thread being tugged through my numbed flesh, a strange little drag that sparked a flashback in my memory, and I realized I was paying the price for an earlier incident in my life, an accident I was responsible for that broke somebody else's nose.

That had been five years before. I was living in Venezuela, where I'd gone to help my oldest friend, Gustavo, start a business and get his head clear of a messy divorce. We were on Isla Margarita, which lies off the mainland in the eastern Caribbean. Margarita Island. In Spanish it means "Pearl Island," but in English it sounds like a bar, some wasted Jimmy Buffett purgatory. Back then it was a tax-free port, so people went there for the cheap liquor and cigarettes and to lounge on beaches of sugary sand and shimmering, turquoise waters. I was working on the beach, renting Jet Skis to the tourists. I didn't really like doing it—polluting the water and making all that noise—but there was some money in it and I liked being in the sea all day. You can imagine the scene. Beautiful girls of every color, greased up and broiling by the sea in bikinis—a spectacular array of breasts and buttocks and legs and limbs rotating slowly in the sunlight. I used to call it Satan's rotisserie. There were men, too, mostly classic South American types with oiled, short black hair, Speedos, and gold chains, preening and smoking the weak local cigarettes while chattering into cell phones. All those tourists, bored, horny, and drinking.

When the rentals were slow, I'd go around the beach, walk up to the girls, and say, "Wanna go for a ride on the Jet Ski, baby?" In Spanish they're called *motos de agua*, which means water motorcycles, and they're as good a pickup toy as their land equivalents. Put a big, vibrating machine between a girl's legs and go fast, with water splashing everywhere, breasts bouncing up and down, giggling and screaming; it's like riding a motorcycle naked in water. Not bad, really. I could feel their nipples harden against my back like clockwork. And I looked good back then; I was tan, muscled, with long hair and a beautiful nose, like some second-rate ancient Greek sea god—half fish, half man—washed up out of the waves and looking to abduct a maiden.

One day I met a French girl who was around on vacation. Her name was Céline. Every day she sat on the beach alone eating oysters and watching the sea. Once or twice I took her out for a ride. After a few days, I invited her back to a place we could stay at near the beach. She was a bit of a pothead, so we got stoned, drank rum, and listened to salsa on the radio. The combination started making her hips move, and soon she wanted to go dancing—not to a big disco in town, more some local-style place in her imagination, where shiny white girls normally wouldn't go by themselves, full of sultry, dark-skinned local boys sleek with musk and libido. We were already a bit high and drunk, and at that time I had stopped wearing contact lenses or glasses. I had this idea that I could make my eyes heal themselves in the sun and the sea and with no reading. They were okay during the day, but at night I couldn't see too well in the distance and I usually didn't drive. I knew it was a bad idea, but she really wanted to dance and I wanted her, so I agreed. A classic scenario—man led by booze and cock to catastrophe.

We got in the car. This was a surplus U.S. Army jeep, 1973. No key. You started it by stepping on a button on the floor behind the accelerator. It was a great old car, but it had no seat belts and everything on it was made of metal. It was also flat and shallow, so you didn't really sit in it so much as on it. What used to be called a death trap. We were driving along a pitch-black country road and the car died, as if it had run out of gas, but I knew it had plenty. It was dark and I had no tools, not even a light to look under the hood and try to see what was wrong, so we were stranded. It was a little embarrassing—textbook masculine inadequacy in front of Céline. Then a man pulled up in an old pickup truck, materializing out of nowhere, and asked me in the thick Margarita dialect what the problem was. He was about fifty, dark-skinned, missing a few teeth. I told him I wasn't sure and he climbed out of his truck to take a look. He had a flashlight. It was hard to understand what he said, but I think he said the fuel line had come off and the clamp was gone and he had one. He went back to his truck and rummaged around in some boxes in the bed, muttering to himself in this peculiar, nasal singsong way that old-school Margaritans have, then came back with the piece and a screwdriver and put it on. Try it now, he said. I did and it fired right up. I started to thank him and ask his name, but he shrugged me off, then looked at me very seriously and said, "You should get out of here. This is a very bad spot. There's an evil spirit around here. Just get on your car and go." I remember how he said that, "Get on your car and go," like it was a horse. So we did.

The lights of the jeep were dim, giving off a weak, sputtering yellow beam that didn't penetrate very far into the dark, but I knew the road. I was going a little too fast, and then I saw the back of an abandoned car in the middle of the road, parked, with no lights on. It came out of the dark like it was moving toward us, too late for me to do anything but fall into that surreal trancelike expansion of time that happens when you see that an accident is inevitable. The moment bends and stretches out like a pulled piece of gum and hangs there just long enough for you to think, "Oh, shit," then impact, back into the flashing speed of reality. We both went flying into the windshield and smashed it to pieces with our faces as the jeep screeched and skidded to a stop. Céline started screaming hysterically in a thick French accent, "My noz, my noz, my God! You fuckère! You were drank!" Some light from the headlights was reflecting off the back of the car we'd just hit and I could see that her face was covered over with blood, oozing slowly down her head like a thick curtain of paint, but I couldn't make out any details of how badly she was hurt. It was chaos. She was wailing and looking at the blood all over her hands and arms and shaking them as if she could get it off. I was confused. No idea what to do. I guess I didn't realize how hard my own head had smacked into the windshield, but I sustained a bad concussion and my perceptions were jumbled, so I don't know how much time passed, but eventually an ambulance appeared. I don't know how. Maybe the people who left the car there saw what happened and called it in. I never saw them, but it was miraculous, because there was nothing at all around, no lights, no buildings, nothing. I still shudder when I wonder how the hell we would have gotten out of there, staggering around and bleeding in roadside dirt for hours. Anyway, the ambulance took her away and left me there alone in the jeep. I watched the red taillights moving away and I thought I'd better follow because Céline didn't speak any Spanish. I started up the car again and it drove, but not right at all, hobbling and shaking convulsively. One of the tires had been ripped off the wheel rim in the crash. I screamed, "FUCK!" into the darkness and slapped the steering wheel with my hands, then put them to my face in one of those gestures of frustration. My face felt wet and warm. I realized then that I was covered with blood, too, all over my shirt and hands. I touched my face some more and it felt like an undercooked omelet, sticky and hot with blood and bits of dribbly, mangled flesh. Then I started to panic, alone in the dark, wondering if my face was even still there, and I looked up at the sky and saw thousands of stars scattered against the black like glowing powder, a silent, country night sky, and then I saw the ambulance come back and they lifted me out of the car and took me away.

Soon I was in some small clinic in a bed in a white room next to Céline, whose face was now wrapped in gauze. She looked over at me while they were patching up my face and I could see she was drugged and woozy. I held out my hand and she took it and smiled a spaced-out, little jack-o'-lantern smile and fell asleep.

I felt awful watching her sleep. The girl just wanted to go dancing and now she was lying in a hospital bed with her face smashed and wrapped up like a mummy. I felt the friction of the needle and sutures pull through my novocained face. They gave me about thirty stitches on my chin, nose, and forehead. There was a deep gash just above my right eye, in the space between the brow and the hinge of the eyelid, caused by a small metal hook that sat just above the glass of the wind-shield and tore into my face when I hit. If I had gone into the windshield a quarter of an inch higher, it would have ripped my eyeball open like a cherry tomato. I couldn't tell anything about Céline's damage under all the bandages.

They let us sleep there for a couple of hours, then woke us in the middle of the night and told us we had to go to the main hospital on the island because Céline needed X-rays. An ambulance was ready to take us, so we went. It turned out her nose was shattered and would need reconstructive surgery to look normal again. They wouldn't even let her see it. I got her back to my place just as the dawn was lighting up the sky—both of us wrecked—and we climbed into bed together. (I only had one bed and there was nothing else to sleep on.) We ended up sleeping together, all bruised and bandaged, and it was actually very tender and beautiful. We were both so weak and vulnerable; we needed each other just to feel human again. For the next few days, we rested and slept together while I tried to find a plastic surgeon who could fix her nose. My face was stitched up and the white of my eye was full of blood, a bright and vivid red, the surrounding tissue gone black and yellow and swollen. Wherever we went, people asked us if we'd beaten each other in a fit of passion. They were hungry for romantic melodrama, like something from the telenovelas so popular there. They were disappointed to hear it was something as dull as a car crash.

Eventually, I found a plastic surgeon who would do the operation privately, for an extra fee on top of what the state would pay him, about eight hundred dollars. Can you believe that? In the United States it would have cost thousands of dollars, and I probably would have been jailed for being drunk and high when we crashed. So I paid, and the French government paid, and at least Céline got a little money to continue her traveling. And the surgeon was really good. In the end—though I know I sound like an asshole for saying this—I thought she looked better. Her nose had been slightly crooked and narrow, which gave her face a shrill, chicken-like quality, but now it was filled out and symmetrical. Not just swollen from the surgery, because I saw her again some months later fully healed (though that's another story), and she looked beautiful. But at the time, when it was over and she removed her bandages and looked in the mirror, she looked at me and said, "You know, I really wish I never met you. I've never said that to anyone before in my life. But it's true. I mean it. And I wish never to see you again." She wouldn't even let me give her a ride into town. She preferred to take the bus. I remember watching her figure get smaller and smaller as she walked down the road to the bus stop and I had a real feeling of ugliness in my being, coating me like a greasy three-day beard, as if my soul needed a shave, and that right in that moment, some quantum of negative karma was coagulating.

So that's what I was thinking back in Queens, when I woke up with my face smashed and felt the same feeling of stitches being pulled through the numbed rubber of my face. Like your flesh is just meat, like it isn't really yours, even though you can feel it, the light drag of needle and thread through a sponge. My mind leapt immediately back to Céline and her broken nose. It was so perfectly economical, I couldn't believe it: an eye for an eye and a nose for a nose, written into the universe. There were so many parallels: the booze, the object left in the road, the magical appearance of the ambulance, the broken noses. It was too much. And I remembered something I'd read in a Buddhist scripture, that it is possible to generate much negative karma under the influence of alcohol. It was something about a peacock eating poison, and converting it into the pride of its glittering plumage, and how the pea-brained bird was an emblem of vanity and delusion. Or perhaps it was about how the peacock transmutes the poison into something beautiful. I really can't remember. I walked out of the hospital the next morning, relieved to be alive and walking, and now I have this battered nose as a monument to my own vanity and delusion. And, as if in inadvertent mockery of my idea that Céline looked better after her ordeal, people sometimes tell me this new nose of mine is cool, that it gives my face "character," or that it's "interesting" and they like it, that it's better than a boring, regular-type nose, etc., when in reality it is simply deformed. In profile I look like a beat-up Roman coin.

CASLI

Why I lived, or didn't lose an eye or a leg, or end up in a wheelchair, I don't know. Pure chance. Or maybe it's like Sonny Barger says in *Freedom: Credos from the Road*:

> I'm not a deeply religious person and I don't know if there's a God or not and at the present time I don't really even care, but something out there has got to control something. Because people can put a gun in their mouth and pull the trigger and live and someone else can slip on the curb and die. I don't think you can kill yourself until it's your time.

As I said, I've had a few friends die in accidents, but the one I think about most is my friend Casli, also from Venezuela, who died about fifteen years ago.

Sometimes, it seems, I go years without thinking of him, and then suddenly, he's conjured up before me and I see his face like it was yesterday—his droopy, black basset eyes and fluffy black hair parted in the middle, his weak chin, the way his head seemed to be perched forward, a little in front of his body. Casli always looked sad—or maybe "resigned" is the word—like he knew we were all doomed and there was nothing anyone could do about it. In these moments, though I never know why or when they'll happen, I miss him like a brother, with a pain that squeezes my rib cage, and I find myself talking to him, so I hope you won't mind if I address him directly.

•

Remember that last night you took me around Caracas, Casli, and we ended up in that tranny bar in Sabana Grande? Such a crazy place, with all the smoke and cocaine and all those slender, sinuous males with thickly powdered faces and lipstick; they looked like exotic snakes in the glittering skin of their evening gowns, the flickering tongues and sequins. I remember one girl, in a crimson head-wrap and little silver bullet shells for earrings, giggling into my ear that you had the biggest, most beautiful cock she'd ever seen, how all the girls there loved you and you were the only one who really cared about them and not just another closet case come around to suck some boy meat on the sly. They were all such hypocrites, she said, but God sees everything. And I remember your sadness about that dick, which was too big for anyone you liked and drew only fetishists and middle-aged size queens who paid you to be their gigolo, and bought you new silk shirts for every time you screwed them. All your friends were jealous about it, but you wished you never had the thing to begin with. We talked until dawn. You told me how much you hated Venezuela, hated the filth, the brutality, the narrow-mindedness, the third world, racist, colonial bullshit. How you never felt at home there. The ignorance of the Latin mind. *"Tercermundistas,"* you called them, "thirdworlders." Come to New York, I said, come up for some first world, racist, imperial bullshit. You'll love it. I'll buy you a ticket. You can stay with me until you get yourself together. I know a lot of people. We'll get you sorted out. I don't speak English, you said, probably wouldn't get a visa. Your country doesn't like us Venezuelans. Commie spics. Don't worry about it, I said blithely, just come as a tourist and check it out. See if you like it. Shit, that cock'll get you a green card in no time. Anyway, you can always come back to Caracas. This shit-hole isn't going anywhere. True, you said, looking off, as if for a moment you actually saw yourself there in Manhattan, the two of us in my place in the East Village, which I'd been describing: the Tompkins Square Park shantytown, the Holiday, the junkies, the punks, the Angels, all the broken-glass and dog-shit splendor. It struck me how you seemed especially curious about the Hare

Krishnas in their orange robes, chanting into the void on Avenue A. There was always something of an unrealized mystic about you, Casli.

Then it was dawn and blue light was seeping in through the walls. Everyone was gone and all the chairs except ours were up on the tables. It was time to go to the airport, twisted as we were, where you dropped me off for my flight back to America. *P'al norte, hermano. Vaya con Dios.* We shook hands and laughed and I said, "Come," and you said, "I'll think about it," and that wry smile flickered over your eyes, and when I looked into them, I knew you wouldn't, but I didn't know that that was the last time I'd see you. Fifteen years ago, Casli, fifteen fucking years.

I remember when I got the call from Gustavo—the classic script. I don't know how to tell you this, he said, but Casli is dead. WHAT!? I shouted into the phone. WHAT THE FUCK ARE YOU TALKING ABOUT? He paused on the line for a moment and went on. The boys were having one of their usual get-togethers: cards, whiskey and beer, smoking cigarettes, the filthy jokes and banter of men who've been friends from childhood. There was gravel-voiced Mario, *el Gordito*, "the little fat one," which was something of a euphemism because he was so massively obese—he looked like a Michelin man made of flab, ripples and rills bulging everywhere in doughy, concentric blobs; Phil Collins, so called for his musical talent and premature balding; Cabeza, for his large, egg-shaped head, always the butt of testicle jokes because *egg* means "balls" in Spanish; and Jorge, a medical intern who for some reason never had a nickname, at whose house, named Luisita, they were playing. Casli was a boyhood nickname for Carlos. Casli had recently bought a motorcycle, which was sitting outside on the street. It's strange—now that I'm telling this story, I realize I don't even know what kind of bike it was; it never even occurred to me to ask. And somehow, I don't want to know. Anyway, Casli was out of cigarettes. I'm off to the gas station, he says, I'll be back in five minutes. Anybody need anything? No one even looked up as he walked to the door. *Cuidado*, Mario was probably taunting Gordito, *o te voy a decir cosas obscenas*. Watch out, or I'm going to say obscene things to you. They always repeated these lines whenever they played *truco*, the same routines, the same dirty, obstreperous gags. El Gordito would have replied with a lewd simper, raising the pitch of his nasal twang and tucking his chin into the folds of his throat like a bullfrog, *ay, Papi, dámelo por el chiquito*. Oh, Daddy, give it to me in the little hole. He'd hold up his hand at Mario, pinching his index finger and thumb together to mimic an anus and shaking his obscene body with laughter. Casli would have walked out laughing too, because that one always cracked everyone up, the thought of el Gordito bending over and spreading his enormous behind.

The road he took wound downhill along a ditch and a stone wall into a busy intersection at the bottom where the gas station was, but Casli never made it. Who knows why—new bike, no helmet, some alcohol, maybe some oil in the street—but he went off the curve into the ditch and was thrown from his bike headfirst into the wall. Instant death, his head smashed like a clay pot in a sack of skin and hair.

No one knew anything had happened. It just seemed like he disappeared. At first they thought, Well, Casli's unpredictable, maybe he ran into someone on the way, probably met up with some chick, maybe one of his horny old buzzards called. I'm sure he'll show up eventually. Then it went to Where the fuck is he, he isn't answering his phone, I gotta go home, and they left, and then the next day, his mother calling everyone and asking where was Carlos? *Dónde 'stá mijo Carlito*, her voice trembling with maternal panic. Then they called the police, then Jorge used his medical access to scour the Caracas hospitals, where he finally found him some thirty hours later, a bloody corpse on the floor in the corner of a filthy emergency room, the weekend so overwhelming they just left him there dead, swept up in the rush to deal with the mangled, screaming people who flooded in endlessly. They never got around to sending him down to the morgue. Just a rotten body: puddles, stiffness, and flies.

I couldn't make the funeral, and I wasn't in Venezuela again for a long time. Some years later I went down for a wedding, and we were all together again. Jorge was now a prosperous doctor with a thirty-foot motorboat, and we were cruising around the waters near Puerto La Cruz. We dropped anchor before a small, deserted island and drank twelve-year-old scotch mixed with coconut milk, floating in the warm water with life vests on and holding our glasses in front of us as we bobbed in the gentle waves. We were reminiscing about Casli, laughing about some of the funny things he used to do, his harebrained business ideas, the sunglasses, his radio DJ voice, his melancholy, and I felt that pain in my rib cage again. At a pause in the conversation I shouted his name out into the air as loudly as I could. It echoed off the steep green face of the island, ringing with the clarity of a bell, and then we all did that, each of us shouting *Casli!* in turn, separating the syllables and listening to the echo bounce off the rocks, over and over. We cried there, floating in the water where the tears could rinse away without any violation of Latin machismo, as if we weren't crying at all, just faces wet with water. I like to think of you like that, Casli: a spirit echoing over sea and memory, mingling with the taste of whiskey, salt, and tears.

AUTOPSY

I once had the opportunity to see an autopsy. By chance it was at the same hospital where I was born, the Brooklyn Hospital, on DeKalb Avenue. I wanted to see what was inside a human body, to see it taken apart and the organs laid out, maybe learn something about what we are. That's what the word "autopsy" is supposed to mean: "self see," as in, "see for yourself." *Auto* means "self" and *ops* means "see," so in this meaning of "autopsy"—"sight of self"—it's the self doing the seeing, what grammarians would call a subjective genitive, because the self is the subject of the verbal seeing. But the word could just as easily have meant that the self was the object of the idea of seeing, the thing being seen, what those same grammarians would call an objective genitive. So both subject and object are implicit in the word's etymology. It made me think of what the Delphic oracle said: Know thyself. Be both the knower and the thing known. Anyway, the autopsy wasn't what I expected, nothing like what I'd seen in textbooks such as *Gray's Anatomy* or Andreas Vesalius's *De humani corporis fabrica*, with their elaborate Greco-Latin names and elegant illustrations. This was more like the gutting of an animal. The procedure was conducted in the hospital morgue by a half-deaf pathologist from India and his assistant, a stocky, thirty-something black woman with thick bifocals who was visibly annoyed to have me there. She had met me at the door and let me in, and as we walked down a dingy corridor toward the dissection room, she tried to discourage me, telling me this wasn't for amateurs and she had work to do and what was I doing there anyway? Did I understand that she wouldn't have time to be helping me if I lost it and fainted like most of y'all, and how would I like lying on the floor of an autopsy room with all that death and bacteria? I said yes I understood and that was fine and I wouldn't cause any trouble, sorry and thank you, I appreciate that. I really hoped I wouldn't faint and annoy her even more.

We walked out into a similarly dingy lab room with steel countertops and bottles and tools and an ugly, light brown tile on all the walls and floor. I guess it wasn't really dingy—I'm sure it was sterile—but the color of that tile made it seem so. Somehow it even made the light look dirty. In the center of the room was a big table, or something like a cross between a table and a bathtub, a perforated metal basin with low rims along the sides and a drain at one end to catch the spilling fluids. The doctor, in a mask and lab coat, was standing next to it and preparing some instruments. He said hello, and extended his rubber-gloved hand, summoning me over. Stretched out on the table behind him was a dead, naked old man I guessed to have been in his mid-sixties or so, with a bloated belly and gray stubble speckling his cheeks like frost. The skin around his mouth and eyes was tight and wrinkled, as if he were wincing in pain at being dead, nothing at all like the powdered mask of repose you see on cadavers in funeral parlors.

The doctor introduced himself as Majee, and in a heavy Indian accent said, "Okay, well, we might as well get to work."

I walked up to the table and shook his hand and got a closer look at the corpse. His fingernails and toenails were overgrown and gray and his scrotum had shriveled up under his belly like a dried-out, run-over toad. Everything about him seemed squalid, inert, and cold.

"Wendy," the doctor called.

Wendy lifted the corpse's head to expose the back of its skull, and Majee took a small electric saw with a circular blade and cut across the bottom of the scalp from earlobe to earlobe. Viscous, dark blood oozed from the gash and splashed in ragged circles onto the steel. After he finished, she worked the fingers of her right hand up into the cut and, grasping the man's chin with her other hand for leverage, tore the scalp loose and pulled it up over the top of his head, turning it inside out and dropping it over his face like a blood-red snatch of upholstery. This revealed the skull, like a large gray egg. Majee took the saw and began cutting into it. The parting bone gave off an acrid, gritty smell, like that smell at the dentist when a tooth is being drilled and a wisp of ground bone gets up into your sinuses. He sawed along and around the top of the dome, freeing and removing it and exposing the man's brain. It sat there in his head like opaque beige Jell-O in a soup tureen. Majee fished his hand into and under it and lifted, then cut away at its base with a scalpel, severing the connection to the spinal cord. As he pulled the brain out of the skull, it made a wet, slurping sound. He set it down, loose and quivering, on a square butcher-block table, where it looked incongruous, a man's brain outside his head, on a table, like an octopus out of the water.

I was surprised to see that the inside of the skull was purple, with a milky, mother-of-pearl-like lilac membrane coating its surfaces like the interior of an oyster shell. The texture of the walls was cool and smooth. I ran my finger along the back of the eye sockets and around the interior, down to the opening in the skull floor where the brain drained out into the spinal canal. This orifice is known as the *foramen magnum*, which is Latin for "big hole."

Then they opened the chest cavity. Wendy made two deep cuts starting inside the shoulders and converging into one cut at the sternum, then down the belly and splitting horizontally below the navel. It was as if she had engraved the shape of a large martini glass into the flesh with a scalpel. Blood seeped and blurred from the lines. She cut more deeply a second time, peeling the meat away from the bones like a skilled butcher and forming two large flaps that folded outward, exposing rib cage and abdomen. These were wrapped in a white membrane that looked like the cottony substance you find between the fruit and rind of a grapefruit. The mass of organs shook like liquid as she moved him.

With the same saw, Wendy punched into the bottom rib on each side and cut up toward the armpits. More dead blood spilled out, like cold, dirty motor oil. She cut across the chest, making a hatch, which she lifted off to open the thoracic cavity, like a small vat full of dark organs. The stench was overpowering, and I had to step back for a minute. Majee burrowed his hand into the cavity and upward to the man's throat, grasping the tubes of windpipe and esophagus, and with the other hand cut them free from the back of his mouth. Using them as a handle and pulling with both hands, he lifted the whole organ mass out of the chest and dropped them forward onto the corpse's lap, where they collapsed with a splat. He cut them free of the abdomen, severed the rectum's connection to the anus, and carried the whole dripping mass over to another butcher-block table. From the strain in his movements they must have been heavy. Moving back to the body, he reached down to the bottom of the abdomen, pushed two fingers through the hole into the scrotum and pulled out the testicles, one at a time, each with a loud sucking tear. He held one up at me and I could see from his eyes that he was smiling under his mask at my disgust and surprise. And it was true. I'd never thought of that. I'd never thought of removing a man's testicles from inside his body, gouging them out like that with hooked fingers. Wet, with their torn tubing and blood vessels dangling, they looked like something coughed up by a cat.

Majee brought me over to the organs, which he began to address, separating and cutting them free from one another, examining their tissue to determine what caused the man's death. He sliced through the heart, showing me its cavernous chambers, which were clogged with a thick, almost black gelatin of coagulated blood called thrombus (ancient Greek for yogurt). It slid through his fingers in glistening clumps as he scoured it out to examine the heart's interior: the mitral valve, the auricles and ventricles, the bulging mouth of the aorta. He turned it over in his hands like a chef handling a slab of raw fillet.

"Occlusion of the coronary artery," he said finally. "This man had a heart attack. Should have had bypass. A poor man, though, no insurance, probably did not see cardiologist. Arteries very hard."

From there he went on to the lungs, which were large and heavy, and had a strange, dark blue color. Again I was surprised. From the feeling of breathing, I guess I'd always supposed that lungs would be fine, like balloons or sails, something spiritual and elastic, but there they were, solid and meaty as hams. Like blue ham accordions to suck and wheeze the air. The stomach was more like a balloon, but a half-deflated water balloon, droopy and loose and full of a liquid that sloshed around audibly. He slit it open and a cloudy brown fluid spilled over the table, emitting the rancid, bilious smell of vomit, but much more concentrated. It entered my skull like a gas, almost burning my nostrils, and I thought I might pass out. Things went dizzy and blurred for a second, a yellowy vomit haze, but nothing happened and my mind came back.

Majee cut up everything: the pus-riddled kidneys, the bladder, the dense, incarnadine liver, trimming the dribbly yellow fat from organ tissue and preparing specimens and sections. I looked back at the dissection table and saw the naked and smeared body, empty of innards and dripping into itself like the gutted carcass of a deer. The skull was still open, with the inverted scalp over its face, reminding me of pictures I'd seen of the gaping, red vaginas of baboons in heat. It seemed obscene and brutal somehow, and I felt numbed looking at it.

Wendy came back to put the body in order for the funeral home. She popped the skullcap back on like a lid, then folded the scalp back over it and stitched it down crudely to the neck along the original incision. His face looked normal again, as if nothing had happened. Likewise she reset the rib plate, first stuffing the emptied chest with a sheet to soak up the puddling blood, then folding the heavy flaps back and sewing them together with a coarse thread like cheap twine from a hardware store. When she finished, she wrapped the body in another white sheet, lifted it up, and dropped it onto a gurney. The hollow body was much lighter without its organs and she wheeled it away easily and out of the room. The doctor snapped his gloves off and said, well, that was it and he hoped I'd enjoyed myself, and was sure I could find my way back out of the hospital. I thanked him and left.

For a while after that I felt a strange detachment which I'm not sure really ever left me. I couldn't get the idea out of my head that we were all just bags of guts dragging around in the air. As Petronius says, *utres inflati ambulamus*, "inflated balloons we walk." I'd look at people's heads or my own head and imagine what was in there under the skull and scalp, the brain sitting in that shell like a giant festering clam. Is that where our thoughts are, in that labyrinth of gelatin? Is this thought itself just a bubble in the muck? Or the torso and foot after foot of greasy glistening intestine, coiled up like an anaconda, squeezing and digesting in constant peristalsis. I didn't know how to think about it. It seemed like another level of reality, deep below the surface. Who was that guy whose cranium I'd been fingering? Was there anything left of him? Would he be buried or cremated? Was he visiting his people in dreams? And what about my father? Or Casli? Or any of us?

EX NIHILO NIHIL FIT

The Romans didn't bury their dead inside the boundaries of their cities, considering this to be a form of religious pollution. They often put their tombs along roads, or at least people rich enough to have tombs did—ordinary people were dumped and stacked in catacombs like stale loaves of bread. And it's funny—their tombstone inscriptions are a lot like ours, here lies so-and-so, loving father, loving wife, RIP, may the earth be light upon you, she wove wool. But there are some that read more like graffiti, and address you directly, though alive now, as someone traveling along the same road, to the same destination. Stop, they say, Traveler, and give me a bit of your time:

SEXTI PERPENNAE FIRMI
vixi quemadmodum volui quare mortuus sum
nescio

CIL VI 23942 Roma

Epitaph of Sextus Perpenna Firmus:
I lived as I pleased, I don't know why I died

quod tu et ego quod ego et omnes
what you are I was and what I am all will be

hospes ad hunc tumulum ne meias ossa
precantur
friend, my bones ask that you not piss on this
tomb

NFFNSNC
Non fui fui non sum non curo.
I wasn't I was I'm not who cares

credo certe ne cras
for sure I believe no tomorrow

respice et crede
hoc est sic est aliut fieri non licet
look and believe
this is it, it's how it is, it can't be otherwise

PART II

ΓΝΩΘΙ·CAYTON

After my accident, I thought I was done with motor-cycles. I did buy another one shortly afterward—the same bike, only faster—but it was more to prove to myself that I wasn't afraid and could still ride, that I wasn't unnerved by the crash. Get back on the horse kind of thing. But I'd lost the feeling and I hardly ever rode, so I decided to get rid of it. I sold it to an eighteen-year-old kid who came to look at it with his father. The father seemed more enthusiastic than the son. He kept nudging and prodding him, eyeing the bike with a furtive, vicarious greed. They left me a deposit, and I promised to bring the bike the following Sunday to where they lived, a gated suburb somewhere up the Hudson. It happened to be Father's Day. When I arrived with the bike, the boy's mother looked at me blankly and said, "I was really hoping you weren't going to show up." I smiled and murmured noncommittally.

What could I say? Here is a toy that could kill your precious son? Sorry, lady, not my problem? The father gave me an envelope full of cash, dropped me off at the train station, and that was it. No more motorcycles.

A few years went by, until August 2011. One night I was lying in bed having trouble sleeping, or maybe half-asleep and dreaming, when I heard a voice say to me, "Alan, get a Harley and drive to Death Valley." Just like that. Not me saying to myself, "Hmm, maybe I should get another bike and ride out west," or "Maybe I should think about getting a Harley this time," but a specific statement, a task, as if from outside, as if I'd been minding my own business, quietly tending my flocks on a hillside, and been called by a voice from beyond. I know that sounds ridiculous, but that's what happened. I was actually disappointed that my imagination had been so penetrated by branding and capitalism that I would have such a consumer-specific hallucination. My first thought was "Ride a Harley to Death Valley? You've got to be kidding me," even though I wasn't sure exactly who the "you" in that sentence was supposed to be: Myself? The ceiling? God?

•

Something similar had happened to me once before, when I was living in Venezuela, not long after that head injury. It was a very simple, elemental life I had there, in the sun and water all the time, bathed in the colors of sand and sea and sky. Everything was clean and crisp and clear. Fresh fish, tanned skin, lime, mangos, ice-cold beer. I never wore shoes. The soles of my feet had baked and callused into a cracked brown leather. Imagine bays with handmade wooden fishing boats bobbing at anchor, vultures perched on a promontory crucifix, fishermen hoisting outboard motors on their shoulders, boisterous women cutting up the day's catch, fish scales and insults flying off their stone tables onto mangy, skulking strays. Margarita Island is pretty big, almost two islands connected by an isthmus, the smaller and less populated of which they call the peninsula of Macanao. That's where Gustavo and I worked. The main island is lush and green and tropical, but Macanao is arid and mountainous, pale and dusty and brown. It looks like something from the Old Testament. The road out to Punta Arenas, the end of the peninsula, ran along the foot of the hills and we drove it every morning in a white '77 Impala with the roof sawed off, which made the car a permanent convertible. Sometimes I drove, sometimes Gustavo. If it rained, we had to go at least thirty miles an hour to stay dry in the pocket of the windshield. Anyway, a few months after the accident I began to feel a strange stirring when we passed a certain part of that road. It seemed to come down from the high ground, like a breeze that got a little stronger each day. Eventually it turned into words, and what the words said was *thou shalt love the lord thy god with all thy heart with all thy mind with all thy soul.* That's not exactly the King James original, but that's how it came to me. Believe me, I was surprised. And it got stronger, until every morning as we passed that spot, it would come rumbling down into my mind like an avalanche. It was strange. Harmless enough. Still well beyond the screen of my sunglasses. I didn't know what it was, but I liked it. I began to love it, actually, that moment in the morning when I "heard the voice of God." After, I'd spend the rest of the day on the beach, renting the Jet Skis and staring out at the even blue of the sea.

Then the voice changed. It started telling me to leave where I was and go into the Andes and preach "the Word." And I didn't hear it only on the road. I couldn't get it out of my mind. I couldn't sleep anymore. Until then I slept in a hammock outside, hung between a mango tree and the cinder-block wall of the warehouse we lived in, and I would hang there with this alien idea echoing and booming in my head, bouncing around like a big rubber kickball, and I thought, okay, either I am hearing the voice of a god commanding me to do something and I should do it, or I'm losing my mind. Let's consider the options: I, a secular Jewish boy from Queens, an alcoholic, sex-addicted, hedonist runaway Greek and Latin scholar, on-and-off-again biker and now Jet Ski renter, have been chosen by a god I never believed in to "preach" something I didn't know—and to whom, exactly? People in the Andes? What the hell did they need with me? And what was "the Word"? Some regurgitated Judeo-Christian mishmash? The Ten Commandments? The Resurrection of Christ? It was preposterous. That's what I said to myself. This whole fucking thing is preposterous. And I am nobody to be getting this message anyway. Which struck me as odd: I didn't believe in it, but I also didn't believe I was worthy of it. And both of those things made sense somehow.

·

One night during this time I got into a little scuffle in a bar with a local drug dealer I didn't like named Ramon. He disliked me, too, neither of us for any real reason—just an oil-and-water thing. He'd come up to the bar where I was ordering a beer and deliberately bumped into me though there was plenty of room. He didn't say anything; just looked at me with his crooked grin and his greasy, bloodshot eyes, and I could hear his mind saying, Fucking gringo, what the fuck you doing here anyway? He was drunk and high, with a smoldering, aggressive glow. It was a hot night and there were beads of sweat in the thin black mustache across his lip. I thought about pushing him back; he clearly wanted me to. It was his territory, and I knew that even if we fought and I did beat him, I'd wind up stabbed or fucked up somehow later, and no one on that island would give it a second thought. So it was down to that moment of two testosterone-fueled chimps staring each other in the eyes, both thinking: Who's gonna go first, asshole, you or me? I stared into him as if I could see the back of his skull through his eyeballs, tilted my head to the side, and with a dreamy note of exaltation in my voice, said to him, "*Sepas que eres polvo, y al polvo volveras, Genesis tres diez y nueve*; know that

53

you are dust and to dust you shall return, Genesis 3:19," which I happened to be reading at the time. And it worked; it spooked him. It must have touched some residual nerve of his childhood Catholicism. He looked at me with a confused mixture of contempt and surprise and walked away with his beer. I was still tingling with adrenaline. And I felt like I saw a door opening, with the voice I was hearing and this spooky incident, a door I was supposed to walk through into a different reality of mist and charisma, but I refused to go through, because I also saw that it was an illusion being generated from somewhere very deep in my mind. I didn't want to walk through it because I was afraid I would begin to believe my own bullshit if I did. Or maybe I was just afraid. I don't know. I couldn't tell the difference between insanity and inspiration. But I wasn't afraid of God, I was afraid of insanity. Should I have gone to the Andes? I knew that if some other crazed guy with a beard started telling me what to do or not to do because God had told him so personally, I'd tell him to fuck the hell off, so I came to the conclusion that life on this island in Venezuela didn't agree with me and I was becoming delusional and paranoid. A month later I was back in New York employed, and the voice was gone.

•

So here I was now, hearing a voice again, though in much sillier form, saying get a Harley and drive to Death Valley. I didn't even like Harleys. I thought they were vulgar and obese, marketed to the most gullible parts of the American male psyche, turning whatever ideal of freedom there was into a slogan and a commodity. The cheap chauvinism, patriotism, John Wayne–Ronald Reagan swaggerism. The suppressed homoerotic machismo. And I didn't believe that God had called me and told me to get one and perform this meaningless task. It seemed unlikely that the monotheistic god we're stuck with would endorse a brand of motorcycle. Maybe the pagan gods of antiquity. Zeus might have ridden a Road King, or Apollo a BMW; you can imagine Aphrodite on the back of Ares's Ninja, zooming around the planets with the tip of a golden thong sticking out of her robe. Even that twerp Hermes on a Vespa delivering messages. Those gods liked to drink and fuck and run around, like bikers, but not Yahweh or the Lord or Allah—strictly black limousines and security goons for those guys. Thou shalt not ride. Thou shalt not be free. Thou shalt pay off the debt of thy sins. In the pagan scheme, you live and die and try to have a good time. You do that in the Judeo-Christian Empire, you get torture and prison for eternity. Seems like a bad deal to me.

Well, whatever that voice was, it wouldn't go away, and for the next two weeks, I kept thinking about it. I imagined an endless ribbon of road and myself rocketing through it toward the receding sunset. It started to seem like a pretty good idea. It's not like the voice was telling me to do something disgusting or criminal, like shoot up a mall or abuse a child. Or even go preach to the indigenous heathens. I mean, why not? My job was ending. I had some money, no wife or children, no one to give a damn what I did. Freedom, the moment seemed to be saying, carpe diem, Alan; a man can't just sit around.

I found the bike on eBay, a 2003 Harley Sportster 1200 XLC. It was the hundredth-anniversary model, with drag bars and a raked-out 21-inch front wheel that gave it a chopper-like look. Black and silver, a lot of chrome, a beautiful, classic motorcycle. That was the last year the engine was directly mounted onto the Sportster frame, without rubber pads in between to absorb vibration, what they call "dry-mounted," so the bike shook like crazy; with the loud, long shot pipes, the ride was a tooth-rattling, kidney-jolting, ear-ringing headbang. Somehow a tiny spider had gotten trapped inside the speedometer and died there. His dried-out little husk would bounce around epileptically under the glass. He seemed like a good omen. The seller was a high school shop teacher in Connecticut who'd kept the bike in immaculate condition, cleaning and polishing the chrome religiously. He was sad to sell it, but he didn't ride it much, and in eight years he'd only put on seven thousand miles. All the bike did was sit in his garage, enshrined like a gleaming idol. His wife didn't like the thing and didn't want him to own it anymore, so I bought it, replaced the tires and fluids, test-rode it around for a while, and two weeks later hit the road.

I rode to Death Valley via Las Vegas, stopping

in Wisconsin for a few days to visit my friend Jon, who had just bought a bike himself. We spent a couple of days riding around the forest and lake-studded roads of western Wisconsin, hanging with relatives, drinking Leinies. Jon's mom, like my own, is getting on. She's eighty-seven now, I believe, Loretta. We visited her in her assisted-living apartment and sat on the couch looking at pictures of Jon and his brother Tom and sister Punk, bleached-out color snapshots of freckles and braces, baseball caps and mullets, blue eyes and checkered shirts against garish department-store photo studio backdrops, dopey graduation grins, all cap and gown, white teeth, and optimism. Jon's first buzz cut as a jarhead. A black-and-white photo of his now-dead father as a young man on a transport ship in the Pacific headed toward Saipan. He's shirtless, squatting on the deck with a rifle between his legs, smoking a cigarette, poised on the brink of history. It's an amazing moment, a young man now long since lived and aged and died, wondering how much longer he'd be alive. A snap of Loretta in a bathing suit as a hot young babe in the forties. She's standing in upright profile like a pinup girl, extending a long and beautiful leg with her toe touched daintily to the ground. Almost seventy years ago. She laughs at it now with big green eyes, magnified by her owlish bifocals. It was early September, "Fall Festival" in Amery. There was a parade, street rides, roasting bratwursts, dances in tents, a demolition derby. Football season was getting under way and everyone was excited about the Packers. The evenings were crisp and cold. It was a nice interlude, the kind that makes you nostalgic for something you never even had. Then it was time to move on. Jon decided to ride with me to the Minnesota border. We were driving west toward Red Wing on a gray and rainy morning, me on my bike and Jon behind me, warm in his car, on a flat, straight two-lane country road with farmland spread out to the south and low forested hills to the north. The rain was pelting and cold, prickling my cheeks and forehead, making brittle ticking sounds against my glasses and helmet. I could feel the wind probing and fingering my clothes, looking for a leak to seep into. I wasn't going that fast, maybe 30, 35, but it wasn't a good day to be riding.

I didn't want to admit it, but I was a little scared to be leaving, out into the road and alone—excited, but still a little scared. I'd had a couple of close calls on the way to Wisconsin, from bad judgment in cold rain, as semis hurtled by in sheets of blasting wind and water. I'd felt like a soaked scarecrow, shivering with fear and cold. Looked like another shitty day, I was thinking, when something off and high to the right caught my eye, a large bird at about two o'clock heading toward us. As it got closer I saw that it was a bald eagle, wings as long as my arms dropping and lifting majestically, and as we drew even, it swooped around and came down above my head. I could feel him over me, maybe fifteen feet, feathers pushing the air and talons rocking like slack yellow fists. I didn't know if he was keeping me company or contemplating a grab, but I felt his presence like an omen of blessing for the road. He stayed with me for a minute, then veered off, careening an impossibly perfect curve and then gone. I pulled over and Jon came up behind me, tires crunching the dirt and gravel of the shoulder.

Holy Shit! I said. Did you see that? Did that really happen?

Of course I saw it. That thing was right on top of you, like ten feet. It was unbelievable. I wish I had a camera. God! It was like something out of a Native American myth. I could see the tail feathers fanning out perfectly.

•

We got to Red Wing and ate, got a pair of imperfect boots at the factory, and said goodbye at the Mississippi River.

"See you back east, man."

"Ride safe, brother."

I don't like saying goodbye.

•

I rode west like a zombie. I woke up, ate breakfast, and rode for hundreds of miles until nightfall, stopping only for gas and food, almost always in motion. Deserted desert roads that stretched and stretched forever. It was boring and fantastic at the same time, like a miniature version of eternity. I wrote a poem on a napkin at a diner in Nevada:

rode on and on for days
through south dakota wyoming utah
the sun and wind reduced my mind to skull
and the roadkill reminded me
to call my mother
i saw burst open tortoises
like crushed oranges in the blood of sunset
smashed armadillos, rotten-smiled raccoons,
a deer obliterated by a semi
my open body flying through the sky
to the fleshpots of vegas

I felt like I was outside the world, like a floating, disembodied soul. Somehow the speed and the stillness and the invisible closeness of death can put your mind in a very free, almost metaphysical mood, focused and detached, while your body seems meaningless, even though it's absorbing all that joy. I like what Indian Larry said about it, "Four wheels move the body. Two wheels move the soul." Or Aristotle's idea that the soul is only moved accidentally because it isn't in space to begin with. The ancient philosopher Alcmaeon, about whom we know almost nothing, is said to have believed that the soul was immortal because it was always in motion; "for all things divine, moon, sun, the planets and the whole heavens are in perpetual movement." It's like you're moving and still at the same time. Anyway, that's what I'd say about it; I felt like a soul, though I'm not sure if that's supposed to be real or a metaphor.

Before Plato got hold of it, the soul was a pretty simple idea, just the formal difference between life and death. It appeared at death only to disappear, the last breath that flew from the body like a wisp of smoke and vanished into the Underworld. There the souls of the dead collected and hung like bats—a kind of suspended animation. You can see this in Homer. A man gets a spear through his chest or his head chopped off, and his soul goes under the ground. There are scenes of dead souls talking in Hades, like Achilles, for example, saying he'd rather clean toilets and live in the sunlight than rule over all the souls of the dead. But it wasn't a place to aspire to and there was no meaningful life there. It was more of a twilight zone between the graveyard and the memory of the living. There were elite religious sects that believed in reincarnation or eternal life, with punishment and reward in other worlds—think Sisyphus with his rock, or that country club of the underworld, the Elysian Fields. But it was Plato who put all the elements together and made the soul resemble what we think of today: a version of the mind or the self, bound to but distinct from the body, somehow both you and not you. Right now it's trapped in the flesh like an oyster in its shell, but it existed before you were born and will be reincarnated after you die, and it lives in its own dimension. This is the famous Platonic world of Ideas, where other entities like concepts and geometrical figures and Forms exist in some fine and subtle way. It's like he made the soul into a mythological creature, a winged nymph or satyr, with a quest and terrain of its own. He even gave it a three-part anatomy. One part of it is rational, one part spiritual, and one part animal, and we still talk this way, even though these terms are very vague. You can see that in the etymology and meanings of the word "spirit," for example. It's a Latin word that originally meant breath or wind or breeze, *spiritus* from the verb *spiro*, to breathe or blow. Then it came to mean spirit as an aspect of personality in the sense of "inspiration" or "high-spirited." Eventually the word evolved and converted into Christianity and English and became something incorporeal: soul, spirit, mind, an entity similar to breath that's supposed to survive after we die, though it's not clear exactly how or on whose authority. But is it breath or like breath? A thing, or like some louche aristocrat metaphor slumming the streets as a low-class common noun? And what about more humble applications of the root; words like *trans-*, *per-*, *sus-*, *as-*, or *ex*piration? Across, through, under, and out breath? How do these simple directions get so complicated? If we talk about expiration of spirit, are we talking about farting and comedy or dying and tragedy? Does it really matter which hole spits the gas? Is the dignity merely a matter of prefix and orifice?*

There's a strange passage in Plato's *Phaedrus* where

---

*Consider the following two entries from the *Oxford English Dictionary*:

flatus: 1. A blowing, a blast; a breath, a puff of wind.
1706 S. Clarke *Let. to Dodwell* 31:

Socrates compares the soul to a winged or flying chariot, with two horses and a driver. The driver represents the faculty of reason and the two horses, one white and beautiful, the other deformed and black, are the conflicting elements of spirit and desire. The spirit aspires upward, to ascend the cone of the universe toward the sun and God and the good, like a moth to the light. Desire pulls the chariot down toward the body and the material world, to the coarsening effects of pleasure and property. The driver wants to go up too, but he has to manage the horses and can be pulled either way. What I love about it, though, is that he talks about the driver and horses as one unit, that a human soul is not one thing but three different animals rigged

---

You make the Soul, as being a mere *Flatus*, to have a more precarious substance even than mere Matter itself.
2. An accumulation or development of wind in the bowels; wind.
1729 W. Rutty in *Philos Trans.* 1727–8 (Royal Soc) 35 563:
She said nevertheless, that Flatuses would sometimes be discharged from the Pudenda.

afflatus: 1. the communication of supernatural or spiritual knowledge; divine impulse; inspiration, esp. poetic inspiration. Also: an instance of this. Freq. divine afflatus.
1736 W. Stukely *Palaeogr. Sacra* 21:
This is a fine expression of a sacred afflatus, and taken purely from scripture.
1865 D. Livingstone and C. Livingstone *Narr. Exped. Zambesi* xxiv. 497:
A migratory afflatus seems to have come over the Ajawa tribes.

I love that idea: "a migratory afflatus"—a sudden, inspired need to move—but it's fascinating how the prefix *af*, which is simply the Latin preposition *ad*, meaning "to" or "toward," can produce such a profound elevation of meaning. How does it do that?

together, and psychic existence is the harmony and chaos of all of them. Socrates is describing a moment of mystical vision, when the soul makes it up to the outer edge of the universe. The driver's head pops through and for just that moment gets a glimpse into something beyond this reality—the blinding light of the world of pure ideas. It's hard to imagine, because the things of that world, he says, are senseless, invisible, formless, untouchable, etc.;* they can't be perceived by the physical senses but are "apprehended by the mind alone," the highest level of reality. Anyway, the driver only has this epiphany for a second, and the chariot is just an image for the soul at that moment, when it remembers the life of its true dimension, where it would live if unencumbered by the body and its earthly impurities. We can try to get back to that vision by seeking wisdom and purification through philosophy. But Plato says you can also come close to that experience when falling in love, when you're hypnotized by someone's personal beauty. That strange feeling of tingling and lightness and happiness, when your being becomes almost buoyant. It's at this moment, Plato says, that the soul feels its former wings begin to grow, when you're amazed at that beauty. And the particular beauty of that person is supposed to remind you of the pure Beauty that your soul knew when it lived before in eternity.† For Plato this is a moment of

---

*ἡ γὰρ ἀχρώματός τε καὶ ἀσχημάτιστος καὶ ἀναφὴς οὐσία ὄντως οὖσα
†I've always thought there was something mildly absurd about the way

philosophical opportunity; you're supposed to use this feeling of wonder to keep feeding the soul so it can fly higher and higher, to greater heights of abstraction and understanding. That's the original idea of "platonic" love, converting erotic excitement into intellectual inspiration and expansion. But you're not supposed to have sex, because somehow that will strip the soul of its wings and enslave it to the body and then you're an animal, bent on pleasure and reproduction. No more philosophy.

Anyway, I've always thought that if Plato were around now, he'd have put that image of the soul in the form of a motorcycle instead of a chariot. The physical exhilaration of riding is a perfect metaphor for spiritual exhilaration because it is a spiritual exhilaration. It was a cliché of ancient philosophy that like is known by like. At this point, though, I can almost hear an indignant reader objecting, "Wait a minute. What are you talking about? Are you saying that because Plato compared the soul to a flying chariot and a chariot is like a motorcycle because they're both fast and exposed, and because you love riding a motorcycle, that riding a motorcycle has something to do with the soul and Plato? Really? Don't you think that's a bit pretentious? And who cares anyway? All you had to say was you love riding a motorcycle; I get that. What do you

---

capitalizing the first letter of a word is supposed to invest it with some special majesty or ontological status. Like a god becomes G-d and suddenly we're supposed to genuflect and shave the women. It's like a kind of reverse idolatry . . .

need with all these metaphysics and metaphors? Why bring Plato into it? Why do you have to make it is what it is into it is what it isn't?" And that's a good point. It is kind of pretentious. A bit anticlimactic. It's almost like how I got to the end of my ride to Death Valley and found myself in the empty, blindingly white salt flats of Badwater Basin, a vast waste-like crust of leeched salt expanding and receding for miles. It almost looked like snow, but it was 287 feet below sea level and 146 degrees. Everything in the distance was blurry and shimmering, but up close so bright and sharp, it seemed to be loud. The heat made my ears ring. It was like a parody of Plato's extrasensory world, colorless, tasteless, scentless, absolutely still and dead except for the intermittent convoys of fat tourists who would step off their buses crumpling water bottles, waddle around blinking and gasping for a few seconds like fish out of water, then retreat back to the liquid cool of their air-conditioned tanks as the doors hissed shut behind them. The only thing you could do was get out of there. I stared into that blank void and asked myself, All that for this? To stand here in nothing for ten minutes? But of course, it was beautiful and fantastic in a way you can't talk about. Maybe the motorcycle thing is a bad metaphor. Maybe the Platonic stuff doesn't work. Maybe trying to update the chariot into a motorcycle just makes it all the more obvious that a chariot is something we don't use anymore, a historical curiosity. But even if the soul is nothing, or nothing like a chariot, at least there's an image of what it's like to be one or have one, maybe part metaphor, part intuition, part hope: a winged entity with qualified access to eternity. It used to be something we couldn't live without. Whether it's "real" or not now, I guess, is in the eye of the beholder.

My friend Daniel, a neuroscientist, says no, the soul is not real—it's been out the window since the eighteenth century when they turned it into the mind, and we can barely even talk about the mind anymore. It's too imprecise. There's the brain, and that's something we can talk about, something we can measure and do experiments on. You can watch it light up in an MRI machine when I show you dirty pictures, the hormones and transmitters jittering across the synapses like sparklers. It's a labyrinth of circuitry, but at some point we'll have it reduced to physics, to where there's no longer any distinction between biology and chemistry, and the mind will be a trackable concatenation of molecules in the brain. That's the aspiration, anyway. He's like a strange mixture of Einstein and Woody Allen, with wild hair and a zany-genius edge. It's hard not to believe him when you see him at the controls of a ten-million-dollar brain scanner at the Max Planck Institute in Leipzig.

My friend Bryan, on the other hand, is a Jesuit. He's devoted himself to the Church, owns no property, and doesn't decide about what he will do or where they might send him. He says of course the soul exists. It's real and immortal, our essence and divinity: life is incomprehensible without it. It's a miracle and a mirror, reflecting the character of God. My faith requires me to believe this, and to believe in transubstantiation and the resurrection, even though they're obviously impossible, maybe even absurd, and I do, with all my heart and soul. It's not about reason—nothing about life is reasonable anyway. It takes a soul to believe in the soul. It even takes one not to. Bryan is such a humble and sane person, so obviously my moral superior, I don't know what to say. To me both of them seem right, but how can they even talk to each other? They're opposing professionals, like a pair of esoteric lawyers on opposite sides of a trial; each asserts his own necessity. And a lot of other people, of course, have no idea, or don't have the time, or don't really care. Most of us even try to get out of jury duty.

Plato had a colorful archenemy in the figure of Diogenes, a kind of antiphilosopher, a bum, or a clown, depending on how you saw him. He thought all this Platonic stuff was garbage and that metaphysical language didn't mean anything. It was just air pretending to be meaning. He even had a special word for it—"typhus"—meaning vanity, conceit, fever, or smoke. Believing in things that do not exist as if they really existed. Diogenes is known as the father of cynicism, even though he had no school, no students, and left no writings. All we have about him are stories of his antics and one-liners compiled from antiquity. There's a lot to choose from. Some people have depicted him as a proto-Christian, St. John the Baptist–style ascetic, wandering around with his lantern in daylight looking for a true human being; others have made him a tramp, or a pervert, or a disgraced embezzler. For yet others he was the one real philosopher, a voice crying alone in the wilderness. But a few things are agreed on. He was from Sinope, a Greek town on the Black Sea in present-day Turkey. His father was an official with the mint there. Something happened; an issue of coinage was "defaced," though it's not clear exactly what that means. Some kind of fraud. Whatever happened, Diogenes took the heat for it and went into exile. Along his wanderings he came to the Delphic oracle and asked what he should do with the rest of his life. The oracle responded, "Deface the currency," the crime from which he was already supposed to be running. Diogenes took this as a metaphor meaning he should practice philosophy. There's an ancient Greek pun involved. The word for coinage or currency is *nomisma*, a derivative of the word *nomos*, for "custom" or "belief"—as if to say that money had value only because it was custom, something people believed in. To deface it would be to deface custom, undermine values, both monetary and social, be a punk philosopher.* Diogenes went to Athens

---

*Some translators say "deface," and some "debase." The Greek word is *paracharassein*, whose simplest meaning is given in the dictionary as "re-stamp." It's a compound of the prepositional prefix *para-* plus the verb *charassein*, which means "to cut into, scratch, or engrave." From this comes the Greek word "character," which originally meant an engraver or an engraving tool, *-ter* being a suffix that means "one who does something." It then came to mean the engraving itself or the stamped image on a coin, then more generally things like "style, image, figure, type, character." The prefix *para-* often implies deception, irregularity, or dishonesty, "something on the side," so to *paracharassein* the currency obviously means something shifty. But why would anyone bother to vandalize or restamp

and became famous as a dropout, living in the streets and criticizing people for wasting their time on bullshit. He seems to have thought most things people did were a waste of time and the things they wanted, like fame and money, or children and love, or even just pleasure, were not worth the trouble required to obtain them, that people enslaved themselves for and with these things. When they act for pleasure, they become animals. Better to be free, not to do whatever one wants, but not to want anything. Diogenes's idea of freedom seems to have been pure, empty time, to do nothing but lie in the sun and be human. There's a zen-sage-like quality to some of the stories about him and his rejection of everything but the minimum needed to survive.

He lived in a bathtub to prove you don't need a house. He ate, pissed, and shat in public, ridiculing the shame attached to these functions. Anything natural was natural. He masturbated in the street as well, not for pleasure, supposedly, but to free his mind from sexual desire. He compared it with eating, saying, "If I could make my hunger go away as easily by rubbing my stomach, I'd do that, too." An orgasm was a necessary purge of humors, just another excretion. It meant nothing. Love meant nothing. "Love," he said, "is the business of people with nothing to do. A young person

---

coinage? Maybe it meant something like "shave off," that they used less bullion than they were supposed to and embezzled some of it. But the petty-crime aspect doesn't fit well with the philosophy metaphor, hence the story's vagueness. In any case the slogan "deface the currency," or *paracharassein to nomisma*, became synonymous with Diogenes and cynicism.

shouldn't marry yet, and an old one shouldn't marry at all." In a fake letter, written later by someone pretending to be Diogenes and replying to the objection that if people lived like him, the human race would die out, a pseudo-Diogenes wrote: "But if humans were to die out, would that be any more lamentable than if wasps or flies became extinct? Such scruples only show the failure of people to see things for what they really are."

The real Diogenes spent most of his time doing nothing. There's even a story that he was sunning himself in his bathtub in Corinth one day when Alexander the Great dropped by to see him, wanting to meet the famous philosopher. Alexander told him who he was and said that as the most powerful man in the world, he would gladly grant Diogenes any wish. What did he want? Wealth? A palace? A beautiful boy? Diogenes looked up at him and said, "Just get out of my sunlight, kid." Alexander is said to have been so impressed, he remarked (with characteristic humility), "If I could be anyone at all, I would be Alexander, but my second choice would be Diogenes."

Anyway, for his various rude stunts and laziness, Diogenes picked up the nickname "the Dog," which was meant as a symbol of his shamelessness. But Diogenes liked the name. He said he wanted to be like a dog: in the moment, without possessions or false shame, with a basic and simple instinct for nobility. A dog knows who his friends and enemies are. And strangely enough, Diogenes was taken seriously rather than dismissed as the insane and dirty old crank he would be considered today. And though he refused to accept students, Diogenes became the prototype for a school of philosophy. People began to imitate him in his costume and habits of criticism. They dressed in rags, wore long hair and unshorn beards, carried a stick and sack, and wandered the ancient world like bikers before the invention of motorcycles. They were called cynics, "dog ones," and the philosophy cynicism, though there was never a school, and never any books. No metaphysics, no doctrines, no fiddling around with math.

His point was simply "no." Diogenes says fuck you to everyone and everything; fuck your ideas, fuck your money, fuck your social class, fuck your beauty, fuck your clothes and your cute little golden boy ass, fuck your city and your country and your religion. There's nothing noble about any of it. We're just animals full of fluids, and, maybe, a tiny glimmer of reason, but we left that behind long ago in the pursuit of property and distinction. I'm a citizen of the world, he said, the original rootless cosmopolitan. So, don't put a hunk of gilded shit on a pedestal and tell me to worship it, for any reason, because it's just a piece of shit. If you can't see that, you're an idiot, and if you're pretending you can't, you're a liar. Just smell your own goddamned breath, for fuck's sake. I'd rather live in a bathtub.

·

Plato and Diogenes didn't get along. There are loads of stories about the two of them arguing and getting bitchy with each other over anything—figs, wine, spitting, flattery. Plato calls Diogenes "Socrates gone mad," and Diogenes sees Plato as an effeminate phony, his metaphysics a pure waste of time. Typhus. The whole concept of the soul and its world is like a parody of aristocratic leisure, a golf club of the mind. Sitting around wondering about the reality of reality while slaves fetch the drinks. Nothing but upper-class bullshit. People have no time or use for metaphysics. Of course not, replies Plato: What would they do with it? They do the work they were made for and live the basic lives of animals. The masses are essentially livestock.

I see a table, said Diogenes, but no such thing as "tableness."

That is because you have eyes, but no mind. Just because the ignorant cannot see something doesn't mean it isn't there.

It's said that one time Plato defined man as a "featherless biped," and hearing this, Diogenes plucked a rooster, marched over to Plato's Academy in a huff, and threw the naked bird over the wall, screaming, "Here is Plato's man, you pompous faggots!" There are stories of Diogenes stomping on Plato's fancy carpets, smearing them with mud, mocking his refinement and luxury. In turn, Plato calls him vain and arrogant, his poverty a hypocritical publicity stunt. And so on. The two of them would have made a great sitcom, like an ancient Odd Couple, the prissy idealist and the sarcastic slob. You can imagine Plato throwing a fit after finding a turd on the floor, provoking another spat about the ontology of universals or the meaning of beauty. Diogenes laughs and spits a tautology; in the end it's only material, man. Just take it easy.

Maybe Diogenes was right, that certain ideas such as beauty and soul are like coins. A coin is a perfect example of a stereotype or cliché, stamped out repeatedly for use ad infinitum. As long as the myth of their value is alive, you don't really see them as objects: they are their value and good for that reason. You could say their Value inheres in them like that Platonic Beauty in a hot boy or girl, even though it's only the mind that perceives it. Then, when things collapse, they become worthless, just inert objects, embarrassing reminders of our former gullibility and failure. And then, finally, a few thousand years later, when it's all dead and gone and there's only a handful of them left scattered around in the ruins, they're recast as beautiful and valuable again, as priceless individual artifacts. Imagine a coin at the edge of a crumbling empire, howling barbarians camped outside the wall. Are they a threat? You're looking at your money, wondering whether to blow town. The optimists hope the civilization will survive. Hold on, they say, reinforcements are coming; those apes won't get anywhere; the money's still good. But the pessimists won't accept it anymore. They see the coin draining of value by the day, an empty little icon of a remote and dwindling authority, a legend, not worth the metal it's printed on. Time to melt it down for more immediate commodities, like whiskey and women or weapons and flat-screen TVs. Enjoy them now, because it won't last much longer.

ECCE PAN TROGLODYTES

Recently my brother Doug sent me a YouTube video called *Chimpanzee Rapes Frog*. When I looked at the subject line of his e-mail and saw that title, I felt some hesitation. Over the years he's sent me a variety of bizarre and disgusting items: morbidly obese people in feather boas defecating on each other and belly dancing, severe Down syndrome children dangling from meat hooks and singing children's songs; that kind of thing. Horrible emblems of a bottomless and depraved vulgarity. Once he sent me something about a slice of pizza with the face of the Virgin Mary in it, apparently weeping tears in the melting cheese. I liked that one, actually. It became an object of pilgrimage and veneration for a few days until its owner sold it on eBay for thirty-seven thousand dollars. But chimpanzee rapes frog? Did I want to watch that? Why would I? Why is there even a thing like that? But of course I watched it—who am I kidding? I'm just the same as anyone.

The video starts with a juvenile chimp in the Honolulu Zoo rooting around behind the glass pane of his enclosure. In the near corner there's a large palm branch. He hobbles over and picks it up, uncovering a frog. The frog doesn't like being exposed and begins to hop around, looking for an escape, but before he can find one, the chimp bends downs and grabs him. He lifts him up to his face and turns him over, eyeing the helpless creature with a menacing curiosity. You can feel something bad germinating in his primitive mind. In his hairy black hand the frog looks about the size of a softball. Then there's an abrupt editing cut, and in the next frame the chimp is sitting in the dirt with an erection and holding the frog in front of himself. His penis is a pale yellow color, tapered and thin, like a small, unpeeled parsnip. At first it's not clear what he's doing—or it is, and you just can't believe it—but soon enough you realize the chimp is trying to force his fingers into the frog's mouth and pry it open like a clam. And the whole time there's a group of children watching it all happen. They don't appear on camera directly, but you can hear their comments and laughter, and once in a while catch a glimpse of their reflection in the glass. They sound about ten years old, and I guess one of them (or maybe their teacher) is filming the animals on a cell phone. A boy blurts, "It's frog rape," and as if on cue, the chimp splits open the frog's lips and forces his penis into the animal's mouth. He begins to pump it back and forth, manipulating the frog like a sex toy. He moves around and assumes different postures, rolling forward, burying his head in the crook of his elbow, arching his back, all the while humping the frog in his grasp. At one point he rolls backward and lies on his back, sliding the frog up and down the shaft of his erection with lewd and deliberate slowness. Then he gets up and turns to face the camera. He stands there, bowlegged and grimacing and propped on his right hand, with the frog hanging by his mouth from the ape's groin, legs dangling uselessly from his soft, bulbous body. It's quite a pose. The children cackle and howl like hyenas. Then a larger male chimp comes on the scene, and the first chimp slinks off with the frog still wrapped in his fingers. Apparently, he's not interested in sharing.

Beneath the video runs a varied thread of viewer comments, which make up a kind of grotesque comic and philosophical dialogue:

Interspecies bestiality and rape with kids laughing in the background. This is disturbing on so many levels that my feelings of unease have become fractal . . . The fact that my first reaction was laughter does not make me feel any better.

What the fuck is wrong with these children? They even understand what is going on and they laugh. Wow! Fucked-up little cunts.

You know the routine: an arched neck, some curled toes, a buttock here, a breast there, a wisp of pubic hair, a muffled moan, another Beyoncé song. Maybe a riding crop for variety.

Grow up, people. When most animals mate they rape each other and monkeys will fuck anything that moves.

That chimpanzee should be put down, euthanized.

Nobody has a soul :)

I'm frankly a bit disturbed by how funny most people here seem to find it. I don't know, maybe some of you who find it hilarious and crack jokes don't realize that something like this almost certainly killed the frog and possibly put it through horrible pain as its organs got torn and squashed. If you do realize it, and just don't care . . . that's a pretty severe lack of empathy. :/ I know it's just a frog and probably doesn't feel pain on the same level or in the same way as mammals do, but it's still a sentient creature. I wonder how many people would still laugh if it was their pet or any animal that they love being killed in such a way. Not to mention the children, who are taught to view the abuse and death of lesser animals as something humorous.

Probably the worst way to die, having your insides squashed by a monkey's dick.

Take your stinking dick out of me, you damn dirty ape.
What the fuck am I doing with my life?
Is it wrong if I masturbated to this?

Carnal desire. Every living mammal lives with it.

Someone should show this to the Slovenian philosopher Slavoj Zizek. He could write a whole book on this and people's reactions to it.

Hitler was probably reincarnated into this frog.*

Finally, one commentator wrote:

Proof that the Bible is real right here.

That last one really got me. I'm not sure what that person meant exactly, but while I was watching the chimp, I thought something similar, that yes, in a funny way this could be a model of how God would see humans, a kind of microcosmic diorama: as the chimp

---

*Thus vindicating Godwin's law, also known as Godwin's Rule of Nazi Analogies, defined by the OED as "A facetious aphorism maintaining that as online debate increases in length, it becomes inevitable that someone will eventually compare someone or something to Adolf Hitler or the Nazis."

appears to us, so we would seem to God, as crude, greedy animals, almost bipedal, just clever enough to abuse one another for pleasure. The book of Genesis lays it out like a behavioral experiment, as if God were a scientist and the humans in Eden like chimps in a lab, like Ronald Reagan trying to teach Bonzo moral reasoning: the test here is to determine whether Adam and Eve can be trained not to eat from one particular tree. They don't need to eat the bananas from this tree. There's plenty of other food lying around. Just this one tree. They've been told not to, and are able to grasp the concept. "No." They've also been told that if they do eat it, "they will die." Maybe what that means is a little less clear, but at least they understand that, if they don't obey, something bad will happen. So that's the deal: obedience = virtue. But how is the chimp supposed to remember all this when he's hungry and curious and there's that one special banana, gleaming like gold on the tree? He's bored of the same old other food and he's not that bright to begin with. Then the female with her big red ass comes jiggling over, holding the forbidden fruit out to him and smiling. She whispers to him in a throaty growl, "Just eat this, big boy, and I'll show you a good time." The whole thing is a setup. What do you think the poor idiot's going to do?

But the video's also like a parody of evolution, as if you're looking back a million years at some proto-hominid using his oversized skull and primitive tool-making capacity for purposes well beyond survival.

It's all there. The subjugation and violation of a weaker creature. Slavery. Racism. Zoological imperialism. The invention of leisure. All the essentials of civilization. How long can it be before the chimp learns to control fire? Or before his brother kills him in order to rape the frog himself? And how far is that from the Trojan War? Or the emergence of philosophical questions among the beta chimps, scratching their chins and musing: How does a chimpanzee's pleasure measure against the life of a frog? Are we not "Primates," endowed, unlike frogs, with certain rights and privileges? And is the frog, now that it knows of love and domesticity, not bettered by this contact?

The genus and species name for the chimpanzee is *Pan troglodytes*, *Pan* from the Greek god whose body was half humanoid, half goat, and *troglodytes*, also Greek, meaning "cave dweller." (The troglodytes in antiquity were a semimythical Aethiopean people living at the edge of the then-known world.) Linnaeus had used this word in the name *Homo troglodytes*, for a similarly mythical East Asian tribe of albino apemen who turned out not to exist, having been possibly derived by hearsay from a Dutchman's confused account of a female orangutan. The name faded away. Originally Linnaeus had classified both humans and chimpanzees in the same genus, which he called "Anthropomorpha." He knew that some people found this offensive and complained of it in a letter to a friend of his in 1747. It's funny to see it in Latin, because you can see the English right inside of it, as well as get a sense of the barrier of obfuscation and credibility Latin seems to provide in scientific contexts.

Non placet quod hominem inter anthropomorpha collocaverim, sed homo noscit se ipsum.
It is not pleasing to people that I have placed humans among the anthropomorphs, but man knows himself.

Removeamus vocabula. Mihi perinde erit quo nomine utamur.
Forget about the words. I don't really care what names we use.

Quaero a te et toto orbe terrarum differentiam genericam inter hominem et simiam, quae ex principiis Historiae Naturalis. Ego certissime nullam novi. Utinam aliquis mihi unicam diceret!
I ask of you and the whole world for a generic difference between man and ape that rests on the principles of Natural History. I certainly don't know any. I wish someone would tell me a single one!*

---

*The Latin form *diceret* is an imperfect subjunctive, a usage known as the "optative" and which expresses a wish that the speaker acknowledges is incapable of fulfillment at the present time.

Si vocassem hominem simiam vel vice versa,
omnes in me coniecissem theologos.
Debuissem ex lege artis.
If I had called human ape or vice versa, I
would have set all the theologians against me.
But I should have, on the basis of our science.

I love it when Linnaeus writes, "but man knows himself," quoting in Latin the famous maxim of the Delphic oracle, *homo noscit se ipsum*. Elsewhere in a list differentiating the other primates from apes according to anatomical specifics like the formation of their teeth and fingers, next to the entry "Homo" among the primates, he wrote simply *Nosce te ipsum*, "Know thyself," the imperative. It's a strange piece of taxonomic syntax. Did he mean that because humans know themselves, they are divine, but unfortunately this is of no zoological significance? Or did he mean that because they know themselves, they really know deep down that they are apes and should not object to sharing the same genus with them? It's as if the words themselves are determining reality, sealing our fate as either human or animal. And even that's strange, because "human" means "made of dirt" and "animal" means "having a soul," so even the etymologies go either way.

Eventually Linnaeus arrived at the euphemism *Homo sapiens*, "wise man," for what he then called, rather unscientifically, *creatorum operum perfectissimum*, "the most perfect of created things." A nice idea, really, transforming a common noun into a natural category. In Latin *homo* just means person, but in zoological nomenclature it seems like a promotion, its own notch between angels and gorillas, hominid, humanoid—not just top gorilla. He further divided us into four subspecies; europaeus, americanus, asiaticus, and africanus, arranged in their own little ethical and aesthetic hierarchy. Europaeus was white, most intelligent, subtle, an inventor. Luxuriant blond hair, heavenly blue eyes. Governed by laws. Americanus was red, choleric, upright. Tenacious, cheerful, and free. Wide-nosed, thick black hair, sparsely bearded, likes to paint himself in complex red lines. Governed by tradition. Asiaticus was sallow, melancholy, rigid. Humorless, conceited, and stingy. Black hair and murky eyes. Governed by opinion. And africanus: black, phlegmatic, lax. Cunning, lazy, negligent. Hair black and twisted, flat-nosed, tumid lips, females lactate profusely. Governed by impulse. And there you have it in Enlightenment Latin: Caucasian, redskin, gook, and N word, born just as *Homo europaeus* was enjoying slavery and manifest destiny. The Jews didn't even make the list.

The name *troglodytes* was handed down to the chimpanzee in his first scientific name, *Simia troglodytes*, coined in 1776 by the German naturalist Johann Friedrich Blumenbach. *Simia* means "ape" in Latin. This was later changed in 1895 to Pan, hence the modern name *Pan troglodytes*.

Pan was the original satyr, goat-man god of shepherds, the wilderness, panic, echo, sex and drugs and rock 'n' roll—think Iggy Pop retrospectively apotheo-sized. Pan was omnisexual, linked with boys, girls, animals, and somehow, both tragedy and comedy. On one occasion, mentioned by Vergil, he even seduced the moon, bribing her with a gift of purest, whitest wool:

> **munere sic niveo lanae, si credere dignum est**
> **Pan deus Arcadiae, captam te Luna fefellit**
> **in nemora alta vocans nec tu aspernata**
> > **vocantem.**
> so with a white gift of wool—if you can
> believe it—
> Pan, the god of Arcadia, tricked you, Moon,
> calling you into a high grove, and you didn't
> say no when he called you.

It's such a beautiful idea, how he could seduce the pure white light of the moon with the pure white sight of the wool—you can almost imagine the tuft in his hand like a foaming meringue, and the moon like a skittish kitten, caught between fear and desire,

> here kitty, kitty, kitty, kitty
> here kitty, kitty, kitty, kitty

The moon was supposed to be eternally virgin, so maybe Pan just stroked her silky fur.

Pan's often depicted with a huge hard-on—*Pan erectus*—chasing ithyphallic after some panicking young lovely, Daphnis and Daphne, the hermaphrodite twins, for example, or Syrinx, after whom the syringe was named. There's even a famous statue of Pan having sex with a goat. The two of them are in the missionary position, with the goat on her back and her hind legs up under Pan's chest, his penis vividly and explicitly halfway into her vulva. This statue was considered dangerously obscene and hidden away for centuries. One British critic suggested it be thrown into a volcano. Now you can easily find pictures of it on the Internet.

There's even a myth attributed to Diogenes, according to which Pan was the first being to masturbate. The story goes that Pan tried to win the nymph Echo, but she turned him away. Echo was in love with the famous beauty Narcissus, who fell in love with his own reflection and died transfixed to it by a pool. After he died Echo became anorexic, dwindling away to bones and empty sound. Pan got depressed. He wandered around the woods disconsolate, stopped shaving, drank, wrote bad poetry—standard generic fare for the abandoned lover. So his father, Hermes, the trickster and inventor god, took pity on his son and taught him the art of masturbation to distract and relieve him of his misery. And so Diogenes used this story to explain his own practice of masturbating as an antidote to the toxins of love.

Plato, too, as if not to be outdone, also made Pan into a symbol, but for something a little more characteristically "Platonic." Hermes, he said, being the messenger of the gods, and the patron divinity of thieves, liars, merchants, and lawyers, was also the father of language. So Pan, as son of Hermes, must either be language or the brother of language. There's a pun involved, because *pan* in Greek means "everything," and language in some way signified and embodied everything. Like Pan, says Plato, language is double in nature, both true and false. Pan's smooth and humanoid upper half is true and beautiful language, and belongs above with the gods. It's the soul, tragedy, ethereal. His shaggy goat half is false and ugly, a musky ass that belongs down below among the many, the cave-bound troglodytes, with their bodily fluids and comedy. For what it's worth, I like to think of Pan as the patron divinity of this book, with its satyr play and little bit of everything, and just as if by accident, as if he were peering out of the letters of this section, *Pan troglodytes* turns out to be an anagram: patron god style.

But sadly, Pan died. There's a strange story, related by Plutarch and said to have taken place during the reign of Tiberius, about the time of the Crucifixion of Christ. Plutarch was writing about how the ancient oracles had burned out like candles, wondering why the gods no longer spoke to us through them. According to the story, a sailor named Thamus on his way to Italy was passing the islands of Paxi in western Greece when he heard a voice coming to him over the water. "Thamus," it said, "when you reach Palodes, announce that the great Pan is dead." Even though no one knows who Thamus was or where Palodes is or whether what was said was even heard correctly, some commentators later understood this incident to mean that the old pagan world had died and the new age ushered in by Jesus had begun; a transition, "as it were," from mythology to theology, or from pagan hedonism to redemption. Pan was the symbol of everything sensual and wild, so his supposed death just as Jesus was being crucified has a certain neatness to it: the half goat, half god, being replaced by a half man, half god. A kind of psychozoological promotion in religious symbology. Others said that Pan simply disappeared, because a god can't just die, and that he traded his horns and cloven hooves to the devil in exchange for a chimpanzee disguise. There was no place left in the Judeo-Christian world for him, so he returned to the wilderness and abandoned us to make rock 'n' roll and wait for extinction. As far as the name goes, I think *Pan troglodytes* would have been a much better label for humans, and something a little less complicated would have been fine for chimps, something like *Simia ridens*, say, or just a translation of the word "chimpanzee" from the original Bantu, which means "mock man"—*Homo simulans* or *Simius simulans* or some such. But you have to admit: Doesn't *Pan troglodytes* suit us to a T?

Well, it was just a YouTube video, a snippet of comedy, a "meme." It's like a piece of dirty digital graffiti for archaeologists of the future to puzzle over. I like to think of it as a rendition of a lost forgery of an ancient Greek comedy, Aristophanes-style, called *Pan Troglodytes*. All that remains is a synopsis, retrieved from a carbonized palimpsest and transferred to video just before the parchment crumbled to dust. The main character, Pan Troglodytes, a chimpanzee, and his frog sidekick, a nameless catamite, ascend Mount Sinai. They're like characters from *The Wizard of Oz*, going to see God, Pan to ask for a soul, and the frog for a proper name. The central debate takes place before the Ark of the Covenant with Plato and Diogenes as antagonists, Plato arguing in favor, and Diogenes, of course, against. The jury is a chorus of satyrs with enormous gold-tipped leather dildos strapped onto themselves. Plato wins the argument and Diogenes is hounded off the stage. Pan is shaved and given "soul" in the form of an asthma inhaler, and a certificate of authenticity written in Latin, "Spiritus Fiat." The frog is given a blond wig and the name Ganymede. He is then baptized, bar mitzvahed, and the two of them are married. They ride off ex machina on a winged Harley Ultra Glide. In a final procession, the chorus of satyrs is circumcised by Abraham making a cameo dressed in a lion skin and wielding a sickle. Each member dons his foreskin as a golden yarmulke and they *exeunt omnes*, davening and singing the song "How Do You Solve a Problem like Maria?"

KOLYA

A few years ago I was in Berlin when my friend Marija was about to have her baby. She called me one afternoon late in the pregnancy and asked me to come meet her for a coffee near her apartment at Arkonaplatz. I rode my bike over, just in time to see her waddling up to the bench where we sometimes met. We sit down. She's upset because the German doctors want to do a cesarian section. The baby is very large, almost eleven pounds, and they think it would be much safer to cut him out. Of course the decision is hers, though they strongly advise her to obey them. It is clear they expect this: in Germany one obeys the authorities. But really it's just for their own convenience, she says, so they can schedule it and be done in an hour, instead of everybody waiting around for nature to happen. They even want to do it on a Monday morning, in two weeks, sure, after a nice summer weekend of gardening in their little suburb houses. Fuck all of them. First artificial insemination, and now this? Why not just get a baby in the mail? Why did she even get herself pregnant in the first place? What should she do? It's really pissing her off, but she feels helpless and alone and starts to cry. Drops her head on my shoulder for a minute, then recovers, a little embarrassed. Could I get us some coffee, please?

I tell her to hang on while I go to the café on the corner. What am I supposed to tell her? Advising a pregnant woman is way out of my league: Do I tell her to have herself sliced open and scarred for life and never know the experience of natural birth? Or take the risk and go for it? I've been told giving birth feels like shitting a watermelon—incredibly painful, exhilarating, a torn vagina, whatever—I'm a man; it makes me cringe just to think about it. All that shit and blood and pain. I have no idea. What am I supposed to say? Drugs? Why are these operations routine instead of an emergency measure? Unfortunately, there's no father in the picture and she wants a male opinion. At the café, a few people are in line ahead of me. In true Berlin style, the waxed-moustachioed barista is moving with the exquisite languor of an opiated eunuch. These things buy me some time. But I really can't think of anything other than some inane platitude like "Go with your gut instinct, in everything." Thankfully, by the time I get back with the coffees and she's stirring sugar into the froth of her cappuccino, she's already made up her mind. She'll listen to the doctors. That is what her best friend, also named Maria, told her to do, and Maria would accompany her through the procedure. But Marija thanked me for listening. No problem, I say, relieved to be off the hook so easily. Somehow we both felt better. It was a Wednesday afternoon in early July. The trees in the little park of Arkonaplatz were in full bloom, and the wind blew through them in sweeping gusts of sunlight. Endless blue sky above. Children scurrying around, laughing and gurgling.

"Don't worry," I said, "soon you'll be sitting here and your own little monkey will be running around there in the grass with the rest of them."

At six a.m. the following Saturday, I was still sleeping when my phone rang. Marija's name appeared on the display. It couldn't be good news.

"Hey, Marija, what's up?" I answered groggily. "You okay?"

"Not really, Alan," she said, "my water is broken. Maria doesn't answer the phone. The bitch must be sleeping. We were out pretty late and she was drunk. Can you help me to get to hospital? I'm sorry, but I don't know who else to call, and I'm quite nervous."

"Okay. I'll be right over."

Twenty minutes later I'm at her apartment, fetching towels to soak up her leaking fluids and packing an overnight bag for the hospital. Saying calming things, acting like everything's normal, and I suppose, in a way, it is. She's lying on her side, distressed and enormous, like a disabled cow, floral yellow housedress hiked up over a triple-sized haunch of pale, dimpled cellulite. A blue towel tamped in her groin. We call an ambulance, and fifteen minutes later a pair of goggle-eyed German EMTs in fluorescent orange jumpsuits are grinning and bellowing at the doorway, "HALLO! MORGEN!" snapping rubber gloves over their fingers and shuffling around. They seem like clowns performing some kind of routine. We all escort her down into the truck, but as I try to climb in, they tell me I have to go separately—something to do with German insurance laws. I'll have to take a cab.

I hail a cab and head for the hospital. The driver is Turkish, about my age. I tell him why I am going to the hospital. He's delighted and says children are a gift from God, the highest happiness a man and woman can have. I ask him if he has any, and he smiles and shrugs at the same time. A stupid question. "I'm Turkish," he says, "of course. I have three daughters. Without them I don't even exist." Probably something from Turkish garbled via his German into my English, but it sounded somehow poetical. "How many do you have, my friend?" he asks. I don't have any, I tell him, maybe one day, and he smiles at me sadly. He drops me off and wishes me the best of luck.

Seems like seven a.m. on a Saturday is a good time to go to the hospital. No waiting. The usual Friday-night drunken catastrophes have been processed already and the disasters of the new day haven't happened yet. Marija's already been admitted, and there's a battery of tests: EKG for the baby, blood pressure, temperature, measurements of vaginal dilation, etc. I wait outside. Marija tells me they're just waiting for the doctor to arrive. He's on his way and they're going to do the C-section, but at least it's screwed up his weekend. She smiles. Would I mind coming into the operating room and keeping her company? Shit, Marija! Of course. I'd be honored. They wheel her away on a gurney.

Within half an hour I'm led into the operating room dressed in green paper scrubs, face mask, and hair cover. Six or seven people in the same garb are fussing around and preparing instruments. Marija is on the table with her arms propped and spread out crucifixion-style amid a tangle of tubes and beeping machines that show a variety of electric red numbers. There's a curtain set up above her midsection to conceal her belly from view. She's been anesthetized from the chest down, but is still conscious and lucid. They seat me on a stool next to her head. She smiles feebly. The doctor in charge checks to make sure she's numb and then they begin.

Soon I could hear the quiet metallic click of instruments and above the curtain I saw the furrowed brows of the doctors and nurses intent on their work. A filmy reflection of blood and viscera glistening in one doctor's eyeglasses. Everything is hushed and controlled, the essence of "clinical." Marija asks me to talk to her, say something, anything, tell her a joke, even. She's disconcerted by the feeling of being cut open. She can feel the movement and penetration of the doctor's fingers and instruments inside her, but without any pain. I feel like a car being worked on, she says. You are, I said, a

Volkswagen. Ha-ha. She smiles. Keep talking, please. Tell me joke. Really? I asked. *Ja*, please. It seems like it might take a while, so I think of the longest joke I know. All right, I say, ready? So a moth walks into a podiatrist's office. You know what a podiatrist is? Children's doctor, right? No, no. That's a pediatrician. A podiatrist is a doctor for feet. Marija asks, okay, so, why is moth going to podiatrist's office? That's part of the joke, Marija. Wait and see. Okay, okay. So a moth goes into a podiatrist's office. The doctor asks, What can I do for you? Oh, Doc, says the moth, I don't even know where to begin. I work for this guy named Gregory Olinovich. I've worked for him for seventeen years and I don't think the guy even knows who I am. But I think he takes a kind of perverse pleasure in knowing he owns me, in torturing me with these endlessly boring tasks, deadline-threatening e-mails, idiotic memos about office dress, sexual harassment, ornaments for the fucking Christmas tree. I sit there in my cubicle and dream about the end of the world—everything up in flames, a holocaust. The doctor doesn't really know what to say, just raises his eyebrows and waits for the moth to go on. I can't sleep at night, he says. I lie there in bed staring at the ceiling, my nerves tight as piano wires, my ears ringing, this endless rotten noise in my head. I can't believe this is what my life has become. I'm so fucking bored it's driving me crazy. How did I get here? Is this all there is? What am I doing here? I look at the fat, ugly old moth lying there next to me in the bed and I wonder what happened to that slender young moth I married years ago? With whom I shared such hopes and dreams for the future? I see her lying there, snoring and farting, dull with age, and I'm disgusted. Believe me, I know I'm no prize either, my teeth are yellow, some of them almost black, the scabs on my head, the hemorrhoids—I'm disgusted with the both of us. We're both lazy, decaying slobs. Finally, after hours of tossing and turning, I go down to the kitchen to make myself a cup of coffee and stare out the window, a moment's peace, until my teenage son Alexendra comes in looking to stuff his face with some sugary garbage his mother's bought for him. Cereal that smells like candy. I watch him eat and hear the sound of the food crunching and sloshing around in his jowls. He's like a pig. I see the same greed and cowardice in his face that I see in my own when I look at myself in the mirror and shave every morning. Sometimes I think, my God, why don't I just end this? Why don't I take that pistol I keep in the drawer of my bedside table, stick it in my mouth, and blow the back of my miserable moth head right off. Splatter it all over the room. Give that snuffling wife of mine something to think about. How's that for an alarm clock, honey? You with me? Marija's a little surprised by the story, but it seems to be keeping her mind off the surgery and she nods with a frowning smile. Don't worry, I tell her, it's almost over. So the podiatrist says to the moth, that sounds terrible, but I don't think you need to see a podiatrist.

I think you need a psychiatrist. But I have to ask you, why did you come in here? And the moth looks up at the doctor a bit confused and says . . .

Just at that moment we hear the sharp cry of a baby. A sound that makes you inhale with amazement. Both of us start crying. A nurse comes around the curtain to show Marija her son. He's big, screaming, purple, swollen, covered in bright, candy-apple blood and a milky yellow slime like he was dipped in a bucket of yogurt. He's beautiful. Marija's face melts into a pond of joy and relief. The nurse disappears and after a minute she brings him back, cleaned up a little and wrapped in cloth, and lays him down on the table next to Marija's head. Her smile is like a rainbow as she caresses the baby's cheek with the tip of her index finger, cooing and murmuring. The instant of motherhood. The baby's eyes are clamped shut. Marija strokes his cheek, stunned with happiness, but she's lost a lot of blood. Suddenly, she gets woozy and nauseated, thinks she might throw up. The anesthesiologist puts a bucket by her head and injects something into the tube going into her hand. She passes out. It goes quiet. Marija's sleeping. The baby's squirming quietly like a caterpillar. I'm sitting there making sure he doesn't roll off the corner of the table. Machines beep and the doctors stitch her up. Outside the window it's windy and raining, trees whipping around in the white wet light.

When the doctors finish, they have to take Marija away and clean her up, so they move me and the baby into a small side room to wait. I have him in my arms, this ten-minute-old human. He begins to sputter and writhe, like he might start crying, and it seems to me that my one job in the world right then is to prevent that, to keep him calm and pacified. I'm not sure why I feel the need to do this—who cares if the thing cries? He's sure going to be doing enough of it for the next few years, and he's not mine, but it's not open to reason. It's a visceral necessity, some dormant paternal instinct buried somewhere deep, even in my burned-out cortex. Who am I to argue? So I sing to him in a low voice, holding him close to my chest and high, near my vocal cords, and the vibration seems to soothe him somehow. I sing him Leonard Cohen's song "I'm Your Man," and he sinks back into sleep while I rock him gently and grumble the lyrics into the tiny pink question mark of his ear. I don't know how long we were in there. The nurse comes in and says Marija's now settled in her room and ready to receive him, and she leads us over. I hand him to her and my brief moment of substitute fathering is over. She brings him to her breast and he starts feeding immediately, without even opening his eyes. The instant of boyhood. The other Maria arrives, a little embarrassed and jealous that I was there instead of her. But she and Marija are close as sisters, and she runs right over to the bed-side. I say goodbye and leave the two of them to hover and coo around the baby, deep in a huddle of nur-turing. I walked out of the hospital into the rain-bright afternoon and got onto the tram. As it clattered and screeched down the hill, a poem of Ikkyū came into my head:

> we live in a cage of light
> an amazing cage
> animals animals endlessly